Circus Psychology

The lives of circus artists can be mentally and physically demanding. *Circus Psychology: An Applied Guide to Thriving Under the Big Top* is an evidence-based guide to nurturing the mental health of circus artists while enabling them to perform at the peak of their capacities.

This book is organised into three accessible sections: mental health in circus, optimising the circus environment to facilitate thriving, and mental skills for thriving in circus. The first section introduces general mental health concepts, and provides insight into the mental health of circus artists, the stress process, and the role of psychological resilience and perfectionism in mental health. The second section offers insight into motivation and engagement in circus, the features of a psychologically safe circus environment, and advice on psychologically supportive talent development environment. The final section explains, applies, and provides practice material for mental skills, including goal setting, self-talk, mental imagery, arousal regulation, and visual anticipation.

Written by Dr Fleur van Rens, a circus artist and lecturer in sport psychology, this book is an essential resource for those passionate about the mental health of amateurs and professionals in the circus industry.

Dr Fleur van Rens is a circus artist and a lecturer in sports psychology at Murdoch University in Perth, Australia.

Circus Psychology
An Applied Guide to Thriving Under the Big Top

Dr Fleur van Rens

LONDON AND NEW YORK

First published 2023
by Routledge
4 Park Square, Milton Park, Abingdon, Oxon OX14 4RN

and by Routledge
605 Third Avenue, New York, NY 10158

Routledge is an imprint of the Taylor & Francis Group, an informa business

British Library Cataloguing-in-Publication Data
A catalogue record for this book is available from the British Library

Library of Congress Cataloging-in-Publication Data
Names: Van Rens, Fleur, author.
Title: Circus psychology : an applied guide to thriving under the big
top / Fleur van Rens.
Description: Abingdon, Oxon ; New York, NY : Routledge, 2023. |
Includes bibliographical references and index.
Identifiers: LCCN 2022018105 (print) | LCCN 2022018106 (ebook) |
ISBN 9781032266343 (hardback) | ISBN 9781032266435 (paperback) |
ISBN 9781003289227 (ebook)
Subjects: LCSH: Circus performers—Mental health. | Circus
performers—Psychology. | Circus—Psychological aspects.
Classification: LCC GV1826 .V36 2023 (print) | LCC GV1826
(ebook) | DDC 791.3092—dc23/eng/20220624
LC record available at https://lccn.loc.gov/2022018105
LC ebook record available at https://lccn.loc.gov/2022018106

ISBN: 9781032266343 (hbk)
ISBN: 9781032266435 (pbk)
ISBN: 9781003289227 (ebk)

DOI: 10.4324/9781003289227

Typeset in Times New Roman
by codeMantra

Contents

Figures

Tables

Boxes

About the author and illustrator

Dr Fleur van Rens is a lecturer in sports psychology at Murdoch University, Perth, Australia. She is passionate about investigating, teaching, creating, and implementing evidence-based programmes that support the mental health of circus artists throughout their lifespan. Fleur encourages circus artists to continuously develop their mental skills, so that they feel empowered to pursue their ambitions. Fleur is originally from the Netherlands, and she has travelled the world to learn as much as possible about psychology. She obtained a bachelor of science degree, two master of science degrees, and a doctor of philosophy degree in psychology from Utrecht University, Bangor University, Tilburg University, and Victoria University, respectively. Fleur is a Mental Health First Aid Australia accredited instructor, and has published her research in international peer-reviewed scientific journals such as *Psychology of Sport and Exercise, Psychology of Aesthetics, Creativity, and the Arts*, and the *Journal of Applied Sport Psychology*. Fleur spends her free time under the big top; her favourite circus disciplines to train are Chinese pole and lyra.

Sharon Krisanovski is an illustrator, architect, and aerial yoga instructor in Perth, Australia. Sharon's passion for wellness and empowerment is grounded in her Italian and Russian roots, and nurtured by her travels around the world. In her illustrations, Sharon captures strength, elegance, and human connection with artistic flair. Sharon's favourite circus disciplines to train are aerial silks and lyra.

Preface

The circus is a mesmerising place, where spectators watch highly trained artists perform a wide range of astonishing skills. Aerialists may be suspended metres above the stage, dangling from a range of objects such as lyras, silks, trapezes, cubes, straps, and chains. Floor acrobats trick and tumble on the stage, while contortionists bend and fold their bodies in ways that seem impossible. Equilibrists show exquisite balancing skills, some balance on their hands, while others balance on an apparatus such as a tightwire or unicycle. With their bodies, object manipulators control a range of things such as a stack of hula hoops, knives, and juggling balls. And the clowns, make sure that everybody in the audience cracks a smile and feels an emotional connection to the show. Although these circus disciplines might seem very different, they have a lot in common. Most circus artists perform physically and mentally challenging skills, often in front of a live audience. From a physical perspective, circus artists work in extreme ranges of physical strength and flexibility. From a mental perspective, circus artists deal with performance, organisational, and personal stressors. Being a circus artist can be challenging and is much more than 'just clowning around'.

The purpose of this book is to provide a practical guide to thriving under the big top, which will facilitate the mental health and performance of circus artists. This evidence-based book presents new research findings and provides novel perspectives on thriving in circus based on established research findings. The journey starts in the first section of the book, which provides foundational knowledge about mental health and discusses the mental health of circus artists and the role of stress in relation to mental health and performance in circus. The second section of the book focusses on ways in which the circus environment can be optimised to facilitate thriving under the big top. This section covers nurturing the motivation of circus artists, guidance on building a circus environment that facilitates psychological well-being, and sustainable circus talent development. The final section of this book aims to equip circus artists with mental skills that facilitate thriving. These skills include goal setting and self-talk, mental imagery, arousal-regulation strategies, and psycho-perceptual motor skills.

The content of this book is intended for general information purposes only. If you or someone you know is experiencing mental health problems, I recommend seeking help from mental health professionals such as a general practitioner (GP), a psychologist, or a psychiatrist. If you or someone you know requires urgent support, I recommend you contact a helpline. The contact details of key helplines in Australia, Canada, China, New Zealand, Russia, the United Kingdom, and the United States of America are listed below (information accurate on 22 February 2022).

- Australia: contact Beyondblue by calling 1300 22 4636, or call Lifeline on 1300 13 11 14
- Canada: contact CMHA by calling 1-833-456-4566 or in QC 1-866-277-3553, or refer to https://ementalhealth.ca
- China: call Lifeline China 400 821 1215, or visit https://lifeline-china.org/ for online support (in English only)
- New Zealand: contact lifeline NZ by calling 09-5222-999 within Auckland, or 0800-543-354 outside Auckland
- Russia: call Moscow Service of Psychological Help on +7 (499) 173-09-09 or visit msph.ru (in Russian only)
- United Kingdom: contact Samaritans by calling 116 123, or Hopeline UK by calling 0800 068 4141 or texting 0786 003 9967
- United States of America: contact Lifeline by calling 988 (or 1 800 273 8255), visiting suicidepreventionlifeline.org, or texting HOME to 741741

If you are in another part of the world, please visit yourlifecounts.org/find-help/ or https://en.wikipedia.org/wiki/List_of_suicide_crisis_lines for contact details of helplines.

Acknowledgements

I would like to thank those who have inspired me to be courageous enough to start this writing adventure, and those who supported me along the way.

First and foremost, I would like to thank the circus community. I have trained at several circus studios, schools, centres, and big tops across Australia, the Netherlands, and the United Kingdom. Although they were all very different, they had something important in common: I was surrounded by exceptional humans who were passionate about what they were doing, who were unapologetically themselves, and who encouraged others to shine. I have received nothing but support from the circus community in my personal and scientific journey, and I am grateful to have found my second home in the circus. A special thank you goes out to the Western Australian circus community, without your encouragement I would have never started writing this book.

Second, I would like to thank Associate Professor Sean Müller, his guidance in fine-tuning Chapter 10 of this book was invaluable. Sean, I feel fortunate to have had the opportunity to work along-side you over the past six years. I look up to your perseverance, your approach to academia, and your accomplishments.

Third, I would like to thank Sharon Krisanovski. You are a great friend and amazing artist. I love the illustrations you so generously created for this book. Grazie mille!

Finally, I would like to thank my family and friends across the globe. Dankjewel mom and dad, for nurturing my affinity with reading and writing when I was growing up. I am lucky to have such supportive parents, and to have such a loving brother and sister in Geert and Eveline. To Sanne, Roos, Suzan, Charlotte, Marlijn, Hanneke, and Kirsten, 23 years of friendship and counting. Know that each of you inspire me greatly in your own unique ways. Susana, our friendship and connection is something I treasure deeply, gracias por todo. Evgeny, Спасибо for being by my side. Я люблю тебя. Lastly, to my dog Ollie, you are such a good boy. Thank you for patiently snoozing at my feet while I was writing this book.

Section 1

Mental health in circus

1   An introduction to mental health

The mental health continuum

Before looking into the mental health of circus artists, it is important to have a general understanding of mental health. The term 'mental health' describes a continuum of mental health (Galderisi et al., 2015; Henriksen et al., 2020; WHO, 2005). The lowest level of mental health in the mental health continuum describes people whose mental health has a severe negative impact on their daily functioning. People who are diagnosed with a mental illness often experience these low levels of mental health. A mental illness is a diagnosable illness that severely affects a person's functioning in their day-to-day life (APA, 2021). It differs from a mental health problem, which is the term used to describe experiences of poor mental health that are not a diagnosed mental illness. A slightly higher level of mental health on the mental health continuum describes people who are struggling, and who have thoughts, feelings, and behaviours that have a mild negative impact on their daily life. A higher level of mental health describes people who are doing okay, have good levels of mental health, and are plodding along in life just fine. The highest level of mental health in the mental health continuum describes people who are thriving. Thriving is a state in which a person is experiencing high levels of mental health and is achieving high performance outcomes (Brown et al., 2017). In other words, a circus artist who is thriving is satisfied with their life, is experiencing high levels of self-confidence, is feeling physically healthy, is in a positive mood, and is performing to the best of their abilities. This book is positioned from the perspective that the ultimate goal of using the principles of psychology in the circus industry is to facilitate experiences of thriving.

DOI: 10.4324/9781003289227-2

Common mental illnesses explained: depressive disorders

According to the World Health Organization (2017), approximately 4.4% of the population lives with depressive disorders. Depressive disorders are a serious health condition, which at its worst can lead to suicide. Globally, suicide is the second leading cause of death in people between 15 and 29 years of age. Depressive disorders are more common among females (5.1%) compared to males (3.6%). People who are transgender and gender diverse are at an increased risk of experiencing depressive disorders compared to people who are not transgender or gender diverse (Freese et al., 2018; Thorne et al., 2019).

Different types of depressive disorders exist. Only qualified health professionals such as general practitioners (GPs), psychologists, and psychiatrists can diagnose people with mental illnesses such as depressive disorders. The most well-known type of depressive disorder is 'major depressive disorder'. According to the *DSM-V* (American Psychiatric Association, 2013) – a diagnostic manual that lists the symptoms of mental illnesses – people who are diagnosed with a major depressive

Table 1.1 The nine symptoms of major depressive disorder (American Psychiatric Association, 2013)

1   Depressed mood most of the day, nearly every day, as indicated by either subjective report (e.g., feels sad, empty, hopeless) or observation made by others (e.g., appears tearful). Note: In children and adolescents, it can be irritable mood
2   Markedly diminished interest or pleasure in all, or almost all, activities every day, such as no interest in hobbies, sports, or other things the person used to enjoy doing
3   Significant weight loss when not dieting or weight gain (e.g., a change of more than 5% of body weight in a month), or decrease or increase in appetite nearly every day. Note: In children, consider failure to make expected weight gain
4   Insomnia or hypersomnia nearly every day
5   Psychomotor agitation or retardation nearly every day (observable by others, not merely subjective feelings of restlessness or being slowed down)
6   Fatigue or loss of energy nearly every day
7   Feelings of worthlessness or excessive or inappropriate guilt (which may be delusional) nearly every day (not merely self-reproach or guilt about being sick)
8   Diminished ability to think or concentrate, or indecisiveness, nearly every day (either by subjective account or as observed by others)
9   Recurrent thoughts of death (not just fear of dying), recurrent suicidal ideation without a specific plan, or a suicide attempt or a specific plan to suicide

Table 1.2 The seven symptoms of 'mania' in bipolar affective disorders (American Psychiatric Association, 2013)

1 Inflated self-esteem or grandiosity
2 Decreased need for sleep
3 Increased talkativeness
4 Racing thoughts
5 Distracted easily
6 Increase in goal-directed activity or psychomotor agitation
7 Engaging in activities that hold the potential for painful consequences, e.g., unrestrained buying sprees

disorder experience at least five of the nine symptoms of major depressive disorder during a two-week period, for most of the day, nearly every day. This means that different people who are diagnosed with major depressive disorder may experience a different combination of symptoms, and may experience this disease quite differently. You can find the full list of symptoms of major depressive disorder in Table 1.1. To be diagnosed with major depressive disorder, the person's symptoms are so severe that they interrupt the person's daily functioning and cause clinically significant distress or impairment to the person. Also, a person must experience either a depressed mood or loss of interest in previously enjoyed activities to be diagnosed with major depressive disorder.

Another common type of depressive disorders is bipolar affective disorder. There are different types of bipolar affective disorders (bipolar I disorder, bipolar II disorder, and cyclothymic disorder). Generally speaking, people diagnosed with bipolar affective disorders experience periods of depression similar to those in 'major depressive disorder', as well as periods of mania. Periods of mania seem like the opposite of a period of depression. According to the *DSM-V*, (hypo) mania can be diagnosed when a person experiences three or more of the seven symptoms listed in Table 1.2. Again, this means that different people who live with episodes of mania may have quite different experiences, and may behave quite differently. Diagnosis with bipolar disorder will only occur when a person has experienced an episode of mania. Because of this, it is common for people to first get diagnosed with another mental illness. After a manic episode has been observed, the diagnosis is changed to that of bipolar affective disorder.

Common mental illnesses explained: anxiety disorders

According to the World Health Organization (2017), 3.6% of the global population lives with anxiety disorders. Anxiety disorders are more common among females (4.6%) compared with males (2.6%), and are particularly common among people who are transgender and gender diverse (Freese et al., 2018; Thorne et al., 2019). Just like with all mental illnesses, anxiety disorders should be diagnosed by qualified health professionals such as general practitioners (GPs), psychologists, and psychiatrists.

Different types of anxiety disorders exist based on the types of things or situations that cause the person to feel anxious (see American Psychiatric Association, 2013). The first common type of anxiety disorders is post-traumatic stress disorder. As the label of the disease describes, post-traumatic stress disorders usually (but not always) occur after a person has experienced a traumatic event such as an accident, physical or sexual assault, and any other situation that a person experiences as traumatic. Also, witnessing something terrible happen can cause post-traumatic stress disorder. People with post-traumatic stress disorders may relive the traumatic event in, for example, their dreams, and usually experience persistent symptoms of emotional distress such as jumpiness and aggression.

Keep in mind that just because a person experiences a traumatic event does not mean that they will develop post-traumatic stress disorder. It is very normal for a person to feel extremely stressed and upset immediately after experiencing or witnessing a traumatic event. If these feelings do not decrease in intensity within four weeks of the event occurring, then it is very important to make sure that the person receives professional help. Also, know that it can be quite damaging to force a person to speak about a traumatic event after it has occurred. If the person would like to talk, of course it is good if there is a listening ear. However, if the person does not feel comfortable doing so, please do not force them to talk and try to protect them from others who are pressuring them to share their story.

The second common type of anxiety disorder is social anxiety disorder, which involves extreme fear of social situations. The key fear in this anxiety disorder is other people's perceptions of the self. In other words, a circus artist with social anxiety disorder may worry to an extreme extent about what others will think of them as a person, and this may prevent them from performing. Social anxiety disorder is not the same as agoraphobia, which describes people who avoid going to certain places (or avoid leaving the home altogether) because they are worried that they might experience anxiety symptoms such as a panic attack.

Another common anxiety disorder is panic disorder (experiencing recurring panic attacks and fear of experiencing future panic attacks). When a person experiences a panic attack, they usually genuinely feel like they are dying. Because the symptoms of a panic attack are similar to those of a heart attack, the two can be quite difficult to distinguish. If you are unsure whether a person is experiencing a panic attack or a heart attack, it is best to be safe rather than sorry and to call emergency services. If a person is certain they are experiencing a panic attack (maybe because they have experienced panic attacks in the past), ask them what you could do to help them. Panic attacks usually subside within a few minutes. Not every person who has experienced a panic attack will develop a panic disorder, and not every person who experiences a panic attack requires professional help. If a person experiences repeated panic attacks, they will benefit from professional help from a psychologist.

Eating behaviour: disordered eating and eating disorders

Just like mental health, eating behaviour is also best described on a continuum. This continuum ranges from the presence of an eating disorder, to disordered eating, to optimal eating behaviour for health (Wells et al., 2020). Disordered eating is different from eating disorders because it refers to situations in which a person engages regularly in disordered eating behaviours, such as restrictive eating, skipping meals, or compulsive eating, but does not meet the full criteria to be diagnosed with an eating disorder. Both eating disorders and disordered eating can have a negative impact on a person's physical and mental health (Mountjoy et al., 2018), but the risk and intensity of this negative impact is larger for eating disorders compared with disordered eating. For people with eating disorders and disordered eating, it can be very useful to work with a dietician or qualified nutritionist. Know that in most countries, people can only call themselves a dietitian if they have satisfied the requirements of an accrediting body that regulates the quality of their care. In most countries, anybody (yes, even people without any education on nutrition) can call themselves a nutritionist. If you choose to work with a nutritionist, it is important to check whether you feel this person has the knowledge and experience to help you with the problem you are experiencing.

Eating disorders are serious illnesses, that can potentially be life-threatening. Eating disorders are not just about food. Usually, eating disorders involve incorrect beliefs about appearance, body shape, and weight. Typically, people who experience eating disorders measure their self-worth based on their ability to control their appearance, body shape, and weight, rather than thinking of their worth in relation to areas of their life such as family, friendships, circus, school, and work. Women are more likely to develop eating disorders and disordered eating compared to men (Reardon et al., 2019), and people who are transgender or gender diverse are more likely to develop disordered eating and eating disorders compared to others (Diemer et al., 2015). Athletes in leanness sports such as gymnastics and dancers are at an increased risk of experiencing eating disorders and disordered eating compared to people who do not participate in these sports or forms of performing arts (Arcelus, Witcomb, & Mitchell, 2014; Kapsetaki & Easmon, 2017; Reardon et al., 2019). Consistent with this, research has identified that disordered eating is more common among circus artists than the general population (Van Rens, Metse, & Heritage, 2022). You can read more about disordered eating in circus in Chapter 2.

There are several different types of eating disorders, which can only be diagnosed by licensed professionals, such as a general practitioner (GP), psychologist, or psychiatrist. The three main types of eating disorders to be aware of are anorexia nervosa, bulimia nervosa, and binge eating disorder (American Psychiatric Association, 2013). People with anorexia nervosa restrict their energy intake (for example, eat very little). This leads to a dangerously low body weight in the context of what is minimally expected for the person's age, sex, physical health, and developmental trajectory. People with anorexia nervosa are either extremely afraid of gaining weight or body fat, or engage in persistent behaviour that stops them from gaining weight, despite that they are of significant low weight. In addition to limiting the amount of energy they take in, people with anorexia nervosa may also try to remove the little food they ate (for example, deliberate vomiting or taking laxatives) or they may try to burn extra calories (for example, by exercising excessively). Persons with anorexia nervosa typically experience their body weight differently to what it is in reality, or are unable to recognise the seriousness of their low body weight. It is best not to confront a person with anorexia nervosa about this, instead, guide them to professional help from a general practitioner (GP), psychologist, or psychiatrist.

Bulimia nervosa is an eating disorder wherein people engage in recurrent episodes of uncontrolled, excessive eating, followed by actions to remove the calories (such as deliberate vomiting, taking laxatives, or excessive exercise). To be diagnosed with bulimia nervosa, a person would engage in this behaviour for at least once a week for three months. Similar to anorexia nervosa, people with bulimia nervosa typically tie their self-worth to their body shape and weight. A person with bulimia nervosa usually does not have a dangerously low body weight, but still requires professional help. Similar to bulimia nervosa, binge eating disorder also involves a pattern of excessive eating (called 'binges'), but people diagnosed with binge eating disorder do not try to remove the food after an episode of excessive eating. The excessive eating does cause great distress to the person, and occurs at least once a week for three months. A person with binge eating disorder will also benefit from professional help from a GP, psychologist, or psychiatrist.

As a sidenote, for pre-menopausal persons with a uterus, it is important to be aware of amenorrhea, which is the absence or loss of menstruation. This can be a side-effect of an eating disorder, but can also occur when there is an imbalance between energy intake and energy expenditure (for example, energy intake is too low to sustain the body due to high levels of circus training). Amenorrhea can be experienced by amateur circus artists and professionals. People who are experiencing amenorrhea are recommended to visit their GP to identify the cause of their amenorrhea. If it is indeed caused by an imbalance between energy intake and energy expenditure, the person will likely be recommended to work with a dietician or qualified nutritionist so that they can develop a nutritional plan that optimises their health.

Support for people who are experiencing mental health problems

Just like with physical illnesses, the right (medical) care can make a big difference in the recovery and well-being of a person who experiences mental health problems. There are differences in the support systems available dependent on the country you are residing in/travelling across. Generally speaking, professional help to people who are experiencing mental health problems should be provided by licensed professionals. If you or someone you know is experiencing mental health problems, your GP is a great starting point to receive professional help from. GPs are medical doctors who can diagnose mental illnesses, rule out other possible causes of the symptoms experienced (physical causes such as thyroid functioning), and can prescribe medication or therapy sessions. GPs might refer the person to another professional, such as a psychiatrist or psychologist, or may be able to treat a person with a mental illness themselves.

Psychiatrists are also medical doctors; they specialise in the treatment of mental illnesses. They usually work with clients who experience severe types of mental illnesses, or clients with long-lasting mental illnesses. Psychiatrists can prescribe medication but may also suggest forms of therapy. Psychologists are not medical doctors and do not prescribe medication. In most countries, psychologists are people who have studied psychology at university, and who have completed additional supervised training to be licensed by a national psychology board. Psychologists can diagnose mental health problems and may provide different types of therapy for people with mental health problems or mental illnesses. These therapies have been shown by scientific research to improve mental health outcomes of clients.

If a person is struggling with, for example, disordered eating or eating disorders, dieticians or qualified nutritionists may also be helpful. They help people identify nutritional needs, provide education about nutrition, and help plan and monitor food intake. In situations where an eating disorder or disordered eating is identified, the dietician or qualified nutritionist would generally work together with a mental health professional (psychiatrist and/or psychologist), and a GP to ensure the health and well-being of the person.

In some countries, there are also other professionals working with people who are experiencing mental health problems. These include counsellors, mental coaches, occupational therapists, social workers, and mental health nurses. In some countries, the quality of care provided by these professionals is assured by national governing bodies, while in other countries, anybody (yes, even people without any education about mental health) may decide to work in these professions. To check the quality of the mental health services provided by professionals in these areas, it is best to do your own research. This means looking into the qualifications of the specific person you are thinking of seeing, to check whether you believe they have the relevant knowledge and experience to help you. When in doubt, please contact a local GP for more information. If you travel with a circus company that employs physiotherapists, your physiotherapist might also be an excellent, confidential, starting point to get connected to high-quality mental health care. Over the past five years, more and more medical professionals have decided to provide their services online. This means that travelling circus artists can now have access to consistent mental health care, in their native language, as long as they have access to the internet.

Talking about mental health and providing support

If you know someone who is experiencing mental health problems, and you are concerned about their well-being, it is best to either approach the person yourself (if you feel like you are in a position to do so), or to voice your concern to someone who you know is in a position to approach the person. When you start such a conversation, it is important that you let the person know that you have noticed a change in them, that you care about them, and that you are concerned about them. Textbox 1.1 provides an example of how to start a conversation about mental health.

TEXTBOX 1.1 Example of starting a conversation about mental health.

Hi Alex, I noticed you have been a bit quiet and distracted during training this week. This seems unlike you, so I am a bit worried. What has been going on?

Together with this person, you can have a conversation about what you noticed that made you concerned about their well-being, and how they are feeling. Make sure to listen carefully and non-judgementally to their responses. Try not to offer too many solutions, just listening is already helpful. It is important to ask them if there is anybody who is helping them to deal with the problems they are experiencing, and what kind of help they would find useful. You may want to refer a person to professional help if appropriate, but there may also be things that you can do to help the person. Think of it this way, if a friend broke their ankle and is struggling to move around, you would probably be happy to help them by offering to walk their dog or by doing their groceries. A mental health problem may be a different type of health problem, but still is a health problem. Offering practical help can be incredibly valuable to a person who is experiencing a mental health problem. This means that practical help such as walking the dog or doing groceries can be very useful for a person with a mental health problem. Textbox 1.2 is an example of a conversation about providing support.

Finally, if the person lets you know they are having suicidal thoughts and/or intentions, it is best to call a helpline (see Preface), to call emergency services (the United States and Canada: 911, Australia: 000, Europe, Russia, and the United Kingdom: 112), or to take the person to the emergency department of a local hospital. If a person has suicidal intentions, please make sure the person is not left alone.

TEXTBOX 1.2 Example of a conversation about support.

Circus artist: *It sounds like you're going through a very stressful time Alex. Are there people who are supporting you through this?*
Alex: *Well, I haven't really thought about asking for help to be honest, so no I haven't really got anybody who is supporting me right now...*
Circus artist: *That must be very tough, sometimes getting a bit of support can make such a difference. What kind of help do you think would be useful for you right now?*
Alex: *Hmmm I don't know. [silence]. Maybe... Maybe it would be useful if I get a chance to take my mind off things you know. Like going somewhere to do something that has nothing to do with circus.*
Circus artist: *A bit of distraction sounds like a great idea. Are there any other things that could be helpful to you right now?*
Alex: *I suppose... I couldn't really be bothered to cook over the last few days. With all these things on my mind I just didn't feel hungry, so I didn't see any point in making food... Maybe that's something I should consider...*
Circus artist: *I think you're right Alex, eating some good food will fuel your body, and may even have a positive effect on your mood. Sounds like it would be useful if someone would cook for you, or have dinner with you. So, with both of these things, the cooking and doing something distracting outside of circus – I know that being new to this company and being on tour this may be tricky – but does anyone here spring to mind that you may want to do this with?*
Alex: *Izzy, who is in my tumbling act, loves cooking and has been very friendly, so I suppose I could ask to have dinner with her... But other than that, I don't know many of the cast and crew here very well, so I'm not sure.*
Circus artist: *Yeah, being on the road is hard like that isn't it... I can definitely relate. But hey, you can count me in for a morning of distraction outside of the big top. I've been wanting to explore this museum a couple of blocks away. I think it would be fun to do this together. What do you say, do you want to join me? We could do it tomorrow morning!*
Alex: *I have heard of that museum but haven't been, sounds like a good idea. I'd like to give that a go, yes.*

Circus artist: *Excellent! And if I were you, I'd give Izzy a buzz right now. Knowing her obsession with creating delicious vegan dishes, I'm sure she'd be keen on getting some fresh veggies into your system.*
Alex: *Haha, okay, okay, I'll get onto that right now.*
Circus artist: *Good to see you crack a smile Alex. I'm glad we had this chat, thanks for telling me what's been on your mind. I know that's not easy sometimes. And I'm excited about going to that museum with you. They've got this indigenous art exhibition on right now, I'm really looking forward to seeing it. What's your schedule like, should we leave at 10am?*

Cultural sensitivity and mental health: a global perspective

The circus industry is a melting pot where people from many different cultures and backgrounds come together. Because of this, it is important to realise that an artists' culture and background impact on their behaviour and beliefs surrounding mental health (Faltus & Richard, 2022). Most of the information in this book is based on research from 'Western societies' such as in North America, Europe, and Australia. This means that it is important to consider how the information from this book can be used for circus artists from other parts of the world.

For example, the 'Western' foundation of this book is underpinned by cultures that mainly focus on the individual rather than the collective. This is very different to societies in more traditional 'Eastern' countries such as China, India, and Japan, where the collective is prioritised over the individual. Researchers have shown that in these 'Eastern' countries, more shame is associated with mental health problems. This shame may make it difficult for circus artists to open up about the mental health problems they experience, because they may feel they risk shaming their community (Yakeley, 2018). As a result, it might be easy to miss signs of mental health problems among these circus artists, because they may be putting more effort in hiding them compared with 'Western' circus artists.

Similarly, research has shown that compared with North Americans, Russians generally have higher levels of mental health stigma, meaning that they are more likely to see people with mental health problems as 'weak-willed' (Nersessova, Jurcik, & Hulsey, 2019). It is no surprise then that Russians tend to prefer to deal with mental health problems on their own, and that Russians are unlikely to confide in people they trust if they experience mental health problems. This reduces the likelihood that Russian circus artists who are experiencing mental health problems receive appropriate support, which will negatively impact on their mental health.

These are just two examples of the impact of a person's culture and background on their beliefs and behaviours related to mental health. The reality is that each culture and background comes with different nuances. The culture present within the circus industry, and differences between companies and shows, may add yet another layer of complexity to this. As a way of navigating these differences in beliefs and behaviours towards mental health, it is important to be culturally sensitive. Broadly speaking, being culturally sensitive involves doing three things (Sue, 2001). First, it is important to become self-aware. This means that you reflect on your own beliefs about mental health, and that you identify what biases you hold. This will give you the opportunity to consider how your beliefs impact how you interact about mental health with others. Second, it is important to take initiative by trying to learn about other cultures, and asking people from other cultures how they perceive mental health. This means listening carefully and non-judgementally to their views, and reflecting on how these differ from your views. In this, you are not trying to identify who is 'right' and who is 'wrong'. Instead, you are trying to understand what other people think without judging these thoughts. Finally, it is important to develop skills to communicate effectively with people who are different from you. This includes verbal communication (for example, the words you use when talking to someone about mental health) and non-verbal communication (such as your body language, gestures, and intonation). Becoming culturally sensitive will provide a foundation for more open conversations about mental health in circus, and is a process that takes time, effort, and practice.

Summary

- The term mental health captures a continuum, ranging from the presence of a mental illness or mental health problem to optimal levels of mental health.
- The ultimate goal of circus psychology is to achieve optimal levels of mental health and performance, known as thriving.
- Different types of depressive disorders and anxiety disorders exist. They are common and severe mental illnesses.

- Eating disorders and disordered eating can have a negative impact on a person's overall health.
- Mental illnesses should be diagnosed and treated by licensed professionals (GPs, psychologists, psychiatrists).
- If you are not a mental health professional, you can still provide practical support, show that you care, and help people find professional support.
- Cultural differences exist in behaviour and beliefs towards mental health. Cultural sensitivity is important for open and honest communication about mental health in circus.

Reference list

American Psychiatric Association. (2013). *Diagnostic and statistical manual of mental disorders* (5th ed.). https://doi.org/10.1176/appi.books.9780890425596

American Psychiatric Association. (2021). What is mental Illness? American Psychiatric Association. https://www.psychiatry.org/patients-families/what-is-mental-illness on 18 November 2021.

Arcelus, J., Witcomb, G. L., & Mitchell, A. (2014). Prevalence of eating disorders amongst dancers: A systemic review and meta-analysis. *European Eating Disorders Review, 22*(2), 92–101.

Brown, D. J., Arnold, R., Standage, M., & Fletcher, D. (2017). Thriving on pressure: A factor mixture analysis of sport performers' responses to competitive encounters. *Journal of Sport and Exercise Psychology, 39*(6), 423–437.

Diemer, E. W., Grant, J. D., Munn-Chernoff, M. A., Patterson, D. A., & Duncan, A. E. (2015). Gender identity, sexual orientation, and eating-related pathology in a national sample of college students. *Journal of Adolescent Health, 57*, 144–149.

Faltus, J., & Richard, V. (2022). Considerations for the medical management of the circus performance artist and acrobat. *International Journal of Sports Physical Therapy, 17*(2), 307–316.

Freese, R., Ott, M. Q., Rood, B. A., Reisner, S. L., & Pantalone, D. W. (2018). Distinct coping profiles are associated with mental health differences in transgender and gender nonconforming adults. *Journal of Clinical Psychology, 74*, 136–146.

Galderisi, S., Heinz, A., Kastrup, M., Beezhold, J., & Sartorius, N. (2015). Toward a new definition of mental health. *World Psychiatry, 14*, 231–233.

Henriksen, K., Schinke, R., Moesch, K., McCann, S., Parham, W. D., Larsen, C. H., & Terry, P. (2020). Consensus statement on improving the mental health of high performance athletes. *International Journal of Sport and Exercise Psychology, 18*(5), 553–560.

Kapsetaki, M. E., & Easmon, C. (2017). Eating disorders in non-dance performing artists: A systematic literature review. *Medical Problems of Performing Artists, 32*(4), 227–234.

Mountjoy, M., Sundgot-Borgen, J., Burke, L., Ackerman, K. E., Blauwet, C., Constantini, N.,... & Budgett, R. (2018). International Olympic Committee (IOC) consensus statement on relative energy deficiency in sport (RED-S): 2018 update. *International Journal of Sport Nutrition and Exercise Metabolism, 28*, 316–331.

Nersessova, K. S., Jurcik, T., & Hulsey, T. L. (2019). Differences in beliefs and attitudes toward depression and schizophrenia in Russia and the United States. *International Journal of Social Psychiatry, 65*(5), 388–398.

Reardon, C. L., Hainline, B., Aron, C. M., Baron, D., Baum, A. L., Bindra, A., Budgett, R., Campriani, N., Castaldelli-Maia, J. M., Currie, A., Derevensky, J. L., Glick, I. D., Gorczynski, P., Gouttebarge, V., Grandner, M. A., Han, D. H., McDuff, D., Mountjoy, M., Polat, A.,... & Engebretsen, L. (2019). Mental health in elite athletes: International Olympic Committee consensus statement (2019). *British Journal of Sports Medicine, 53*, 667–699.

Sue, D. W. (2001). Multidimensional facets of cultural competence. *The Counseling Psychologist, 29*(6), 790–821.

Thorne, N., Witcomb, G. L., Nieder, T., Nixon, E., Yip, A., & Arcelus, J. (2019). A comparison of mental health symptomatology and levels of social support in young treatment seeking transgender individuals who identify as binary and non-binary. *International Journal of Transgenderism, 20*(2–3), 241–250.

Van Rens, F. E.C. A., Metse, A. P., & Heritage, B. (2022). Exploring the mental health of circus artists: Circus factors, psychological resilience, and demographics predict disordered eating and exercise addictions. *Psychology of Sport and Exercise, 59*, 102107.

Wells, K. R., Jeacocke, N. A., Appaneal, R., Smith, H. D., Vlahovich, N., Burke, L. M., & Hughes, D. (2020). The Australian Institute of Sport (AIS) and National Eating Disorders Collaboration (NEDC) position statement on disordered eating in high performance sport. *British Journal of Sports Medicine, 54*, 1247–1258.

World Health Organization. (2005). *Promoting mental health: Concepts, emerging evidence, practice.* Geneva: WHO.

World Health Organization. (2017). Depression and other common mental disorders: Global health estimates (No. WHO/MSD/MER/2017.2). World Health Organization. https://www.who.int/mental_health/management/depression/prevalence_global_health_estimates/en/

Yakeley, J. (2018). Shame, culture and mental health. *Nordic Journal of Psychiatry, 72*(supl), S20–S22.

2 The mental health of circus artists

Emotional states of stress, anxiety, and depression in circus

Although there is very little research that investigated the mental health of circus artists, there are some scientific studies that provide a broad understanding of the levels of mental health experienced by circus artists. Importantly, a large research project that included 500 circus artists from across the globe looked at circus artists' experiences of emotional states of stress, anxiety, and depression (Van Rens & Heritage, 2021). A person who experiences emotional states of anxiety or depression does not necessarily have a mental illness. However, experiences of emotional states of anxiety and depression are indicators of those mental illnesses. High emotional states of anxiety and depression can be seen as mental health problems on the mental health continuum (see Chapter 1). Research has shown that circus artists experience higher emotional states of depression, anxiety, and stress than the general population, and that they experience significantly lower levels of flourishing than the general population (Van Rens & Heritage 2021). This means that on average, circus artists experience lower levels of mental health than the general population. Looking in more detail, Figure 2.1 shows that 44% of the circus artists in this study reported higher emotional states of stress and anxiety compared to scores that are seen as 'normal' in the general population, and 49% of circus artists reported scores that exceeded 'normal' emotional states of depression. Alarmingly, 13% of the circus artists scored in the severe/extremely severe range for emotional states of stress, 18% reported experiencing severe/extremely severe emotional states of anxiety, and 18% experienced severe/extremely severe emotional states of depression.

DOI: 10.4324/9781003289227–3

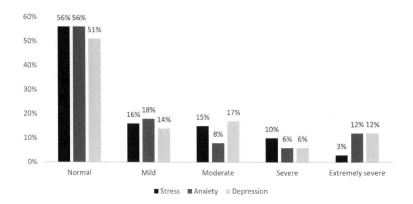

Figure 2.1 Percentage of circus artists experiencing normal, mild, moderate, severe, and extremely severe emotional states of stress, anxiety, and depression.

During the COVID-19 pandemic, performing arts students (including circus students) experienced less stress and increased sleep compared with before this pandemic (Stubbe et al., 2021); however, their levels of loneliness increased during this time, and their levels of general mental health decreased. This means that there is reason to be concerned about the mental health of circus artists, and that there is a need for appropriate mental health support for circus artists (see Ménard & Hallé, 2014).

Research also tried to uncover whether there are any factors that predicted the levels of emotional states of depression, anxiety, and stress experienced by circus artists (Van Rens & Heritage, 2021). Circus artists who are younger and who are transgender or gender diverse are more likely to experience higher emotional states of depression, anxiety, and stress (and thus, lower mental health). The artists' circus disciplines were also related to emotional states of depression, anxiety, and stress. Artists whose primary circus discipline was object manipulation generally reported the lowest levels of mental health, lower than aerial acrobats and equilibrium artists. Floor acrobats reported greater levels of mental health than aerial acrobats. The way in which circus artists participated in circus was also related to mental health. Amateur circus artists generally reported higher levels of mental health than semi-professional circus artists, students at national circus schools, and retired circus artists. Finally, it was found that psychological resilience is related to mental health. Circus artists who had higher levels of psychological resilience were more likely to experience higher levels of mental health. Taken together, this means that there is a complex interplay between personal and circus-specific factors that impact on the mental health of circus artists.

The role of psychological resilience in the mental health of circus artists

Because psychological resilience was found to be a strong predictor of the mental health of circus artists (Van Rens & Heritage, 2021), it is useful to unpack psychological resilience in more detail. Sports psychologists define psychological resilience as '…the role of mental processes and behaviour in promoting personal assets and protecting an individual from the potential negative effect of stressors' (Fletcher & Sarkar, 2012, p. 675). There are two important components to this definition of psychological resilience. First, psychological resilience is a resource that helps an individual deal with stressors, and it can be seen as a protective factor in the appraisal component of the stress process (see Chapter 3). Second, this definition shows that psychological resilience consists of a range of mental processes. According to Fletcher and Sarkar (2012), psychological resilience consists of five protective components.

The first component of psychological resilience is confidence. If you are confident that you are going to be successful in handling a challenge, this puts you in a better position to deal with the challenge. The second component is social support, believing that you are supported by others (such as family, friends, cast, and crew) is beneficial in dealing with stressors. The third component is focus, being able to focus on a challenging situation when necessary, and being able to shift attention away from the challenging situation when beneficial is useful when dealing with a challenge. Also, being able to focus on the process rather than an outcome is beneficial when dealing with challenges too. The fourth component of psychological resilience is motivation. Having high levels of intrinsic motivation (see Chapter 4), high levels of passion for circus, and choosing to engage in challenging situations rather than trying to avoid them will help when dealing with stressors. The final, fifth, component is having a positive personality, which relates to remaining optimistic, being open to new experiences, and being innovative and proactive in the face of challenging situations. These five factors of psychological resilience play a crucial role in thriving for elite gymnasts who achieved a career as professional circus artists (Van Rens & Filho, 2019). From this, it is clear that psychological resilience is an important factor that impacts mental health in circus.

Importantly, psychological resilience is a mental process that is changeable. This means that with mental skills training (overseen by a licensed psychologist of course), circus artists can train to become more psychologically resilient. Although no specific research has looked at the impact of psychological resilience training in circus, research in sport has shown that psychological resilience training has a positive impact on the performance and well-being of athletes (see Kegelaers et al., 2021; Van Rens, Burgin, & Morris-Binelli, 2021). This positive impact of psychological resilience training is particularly strong if there are also changes in organisational policies and practices that support psychological resilience (Sarkar & Page, 2022). What is more, buddy systems have been successfully used to improve the social support component of psychological resilience and have shown to facilitate well-being during life changes (Hughes, 2009).

Disordered eating in circus

Approximately 36% of circus artists report engaging in disordered eating behaviour, and are in the 'at-risk' category of having an eating disorder as assessed by the EAT-26 eating disorders measure (see Garner et al., 1982; Van Rens, Metse, & Heritage, 2022). This percentage shows that – just like athletes in leanness sports such as gymnastics – circus artists are at an increased risk of developing disordered eating compared with the general population. The same research also showed that circus artists who reported to have engaged in disordered eating were more likely to experience exercise addiction compared with circus artists who did not experience disordered eating. This finding is consistent with other research in psychology, which describes that so-called 'secondary exercise addictions' may occur at the same time as eating disorders in an attempt to lose weight (see Berczik et al., 2012; Trott et al., 2021).

Multiple circus-specific factors are related to the likelihood that a circus artist develops disordered eating (Van Rens et al., 2022). One of these factors is the main circus discipline of the artist. Specifically, equilibrium artists and aerial acrobats were more likely to experience disordered eating compared to other circus artists. Equilibrium artists also reported higher scores on a measure of exercise addiction compared to other circus artists. Older circus artists were less likely to engage in disordered eating compared to younger circus artists, but gender was not related to the likelihood of engaging in disordered eating among circus artists. Finally, higher levels of psychological resilience were related to a decreased likelihood of experiencing disordered eating. Together, these research findings show that disordered eating is common among circus artists. It also highlights the importance of interventions that may prevent the development of disordered eating in the circus setting. This includes setting up the circus environment in a way that minimises a negative impact on body satisfaction (see Chapter 5), as well as promoting access to experts who can provide mental skills training and nutritional advice to circus artists.

(Psychological) predictors of injuries in circus

Participation in circus comes with a risk of experiencing injuries. Research shows that acrobats and tumblers are most likely to experience injuries, followed by those who engage in hand balancing, adagio, and Chinese pole (Munro, 2014). Consistent with this, floor acrobats are more likely to experience accidents than aerial acrobats and object manipulators (Van Rens & Filho, 2021). Of course, there are a range of discipline-specific demands and physiological factors that cause these differences between circus disciplines. More generally though, training overload and a lack of recovery are key predictors of injuries in the performing arts (Nunes et al., 2022). Successful management of the balance between (training) stress and recovery could prevent injuries in circus. Chapter 9 discusses how to balance stress and recovery.

Aside from training load, recovery, discipline-specific factors, and other physiological components, psychological factors are also known to predict the likelihood of sustaining injuries. In dance, experiences of stress, psychological distress, disordered eating, and catastrophising when under pressure are related to an increased risk of sustaining an injury and worsened outcomes of the injury (Mainwaring & Finney, 2017). Because of the similarities between dance and circus, it will be useful for circus artists to use mental skills that reduce stress, so that their likelihood of experiencing injuries decreases. Section 3 of this book provides information and guidance on how to use these mental skills. Further, a lack of sleep, high levels of perfectionistic traits, and a lack of social support were also related to an increased likelihood of experiencing injuries in dance (Mainwaring & Finney, 2017).

Psychological factors also impact on the risk of experiencing accidents in circus. It is a common misconception that all circus artists who train or perform in 'risky' circus disciplines such as flying trapeze, fire acts, or aerial acrobatics do this for the thrill of it or to experience a rush of adrenaline. Although some circus artists might be motivated to perform circus to experience a thrill, most circus artists tend to train or perform in 'risky' circus disciplines to experience a sense of control and mastery of skills (Hofsess, 1986). This means that for some, circus helps them experience and control emotions, a process that is called emotion regulation. Circus artists who experience high levels of emotion regulation during training and performance in circus are more likely to experience accidents than other circus artists (Van Rens & Filho, 2021). Circus artists who experience a thrill or adrenaline rush are not more likely than others to experience accidents. Another psychological factor that predicts the likelihood of accidents occurring is the personality trait conscientiousness. People who score high on this personality trait have high levels of self-discipline, act dutifully, and like to follow a plan. Circus artists who are highly conscientious are less likely to experience accidents and near misses than circus artists who score lower on this personality trait (Van Rens & Filho, 2021). Together, this means that we should consider circus artists' psychological resources to help prevent accidents and injuries under the big top.

Mental health consequences of injuries in circus artists

When a circus artist gets injured, this may cause feelings of fear, isolation, depression, anxiety, and stress (Ganderton et al., 2021). Consistent with this, plenty of research from dance and sport has shown that injuries negatively impact on the mental health of artists and athletes (Gulliver et al., 2015; Pollitt & Hutt, 2021). Supporting the mental health of circus artists who are experiencing injuries is thus important. To provide effective support, the specific challenges the circus artist experiences need to be considered. Three main challenges that injured circus artists may experience are maintaining mental health immediately after getting injured, maintaining motivation during rehabilitation, and maintaining confidence when returning to full pre-injury levels of activity. The next paragraphs describe these three challenges in more detail.

Immediately after an injury occurs, it may be difficult for a circus artist to maintain their levels of mental health (Schinke et al., 2018). It is normal for an injured circus artist to experience negative emotions such as anger, grief, shock, disbelief, self-pity, and depressive states. Because of this, it is helpful to provide (social) support to the circus artist. This support can be provided by friends, family members, cast, crew, physiotherapists, etc. Learning and using arousal-regulation skills such as progressive muscle relaxation (see Chapter 9) and mental imagery (see Chapter 8) can also be useful to circus artists who are dealing with high levels of stress due to their injury. Although experiencing some emotional turmoil is a normal response to an injury, it is important to keep an eye on signs that show that the emotional response to an injury is too extreme. These warning signs include the circus artist being in denial of their injury, coming back too soon and therefore repeatedly injuring oneself, fearing that recovery will not happen, and dwelling on minor complaints. Extreme warning signs that indicate mental health problems coincide with symptoms of major depressive disorder (see Chapter 1) and include social withdrawal, mood swings, and feelings of excessive guilt (such as letting cast and crew down). If you notice these extreme warning signs in a circus artists' response to an injury, it is best to keep supporting the circus artist while also referring them to a licensed psychologist (see Chapter 1).

Special attention should be paid to concussions among circus artists. At the moment, little is known about the prevalence or impact of concussions among circus artists (Russell et al., 2021). That said, concussions are the most often reported specific injury among female gymnasts, so it is likely that concussions are a common injury among acrobats too (Chandran et al., 2021). From sport, we know that the psychological impact of concussions on the brain's mood centres can last weeks to years post-concussion, and can cause heightened feelings of anxiety, depression, and irritability (Harmon et al., 2013). Concussions can cause neurocognitive changes to the brain, which can have short-term impacts (such as decreases in concentration, cognitive processing, memory, blurred vision, etc.) and long-lasting impacts from recurrent concussions. Concussions are thus serious injuries, which may have big mental health consequences.

During rehabilitation and recovery from an injury, it can be difficult for circus artists to maintain the levels and types of motivation required to successfully follow their rehabilitation programme (Ardern et al., 2013). One way of supporting the motivation of circus artists during rehabilitation is to make sure that circus artists can experience intrinsic levels of motivation. This can be achieved by using the principles of self-determination theory when working with injured circus artists (see Chapter 4). It is also helpful to set appropriate goals together with circus artists so that they can achieve a sense of progress and accomplishment during rehabilitation (see Chapter 7).

When a circus artist has (almost) completed their rehabilitation and recovery from the injury, it is important to work with the circus artist on their psychological readiness to return to training and performing. It is normal for circus artists to worry about pain and re-injury, about falling behind others in terms of their skill level (and their chances of getting hired) and to fear that they will be underperforming. It is useful for circus artists in this phase to normalise that they may not be performing to pre-injury standards just yet. Some reasons why this is normal is that the artist may have had to adopt different techniques in technical aspects of their circus discipline due to the injury/to prevent future injuries, they may have been unable to train and perform their circus discipline for a prolonged period of time, they may have lost some strength and/or physical fitness, and it may seem that the previously injured circus artist is not performing as well as before because other circus artists may have improved during the time that the previously injured circus artist was working on their recovery. In sport, successful return to competition is related to having high levels of self-confidence (Ardern et al., 2013). This is likely the same in circus. To achieve high levels of self-confidence in circus artists who are returning to the stage of a period of injury, it is important to encourage the circus artist to learn and use mental skills that impact on self-confidence in the 'return to full activity phase'. Mental skills that are effective in increasing self-confidence are positive self-talk (see Chapter 7), mental imagery (see Chapter 8), and arousal regulation (see Chapter 9).

Perfectionism and mental health

Another factor to consider in relation to mental health is the circus artist's level of perfectionism. Research has shown that dancers and professional athletes score relatively high on the personality characteristic perfectionism (Hill, 2016), so it is plausible that circus artists also score high on perfectionism. People who score high on perfectionism tend to set very high standards for themselves, strive to achieve flawlessness, and are critical of their performance (Stoeber, 2011). Perfectionism is generally seen as a contributor to achieving high levels of performance. After all, if artists do not set high goals for themselves (such as obtaining high levels of flexibility, learning to juggle six balls, or becoming part of a certain circus show), they are less likely to achieve that goal. In that sense, scoring high on the personality characteristic perfectionism can be considered a good thing, and this may explain why some people see perfectionism as a strength rather than a flaw. However, things are a little bit more complicated than that.

Roughly speaking, researchers have identified two types of perfectionism (Stoeber, 2011; Terry-Short et al., 1995). The first type of perfectionism is adaptive perfectionism, otherwise known as perfectionistic striving. In a nutshell, this type of perfectionism describes people who set high standards for themselves, but who are not too worried about how others evaluate them. Having high levels of perfectionistic striving is mostly a good thing, it relates to high levels of performance and does not appear to be detrimental to mental health.

The second type of perfectionism is called maladaptive perfectionism, or perfectionistic concern. In short, people with high levels of this type of perfectionism set high standards for themselves, and have a high level of concern over making mistakes. It is common for people who score high on perfectionistic concern to relate their performance to their levels of self-worth. This means that circus artists who score high on perfectionistic concern will think less of themselves after a performance that they perceive to be not living up to their standards. Given that people who score high on perfectionism set such high goals for themselves, circus artists who score high on maladaptive perfectionism may quickly evaluate their performance as 'not good enough', and worry that other people will think less of them. Perfectionistic concern can have a negative impact on people's daily lives. Research has shown that this type of perfectionism is associated with mental health problems such as anxiety, depression, and suicide (Smith et al., 2021).

You might wonder what you can do if perfectionistic concern stands in the way of someone's happiness. Goal-setting skills could help circus artists who score high on perfectionistic concern (see Chapter 7). These include setting small goals and celebrating successes. You juggled six balls for the first time? Reward yourself! You overcame your fear and auditioned for a show? That is awesome! It is also helpful to adjust goals when necessary because you cannot predict everything in life. You may be working with an injury, or may be on a strange sleeping schedule. This may affect your abilities during training or on stage. Keep this in mind when setting your goals for the day. It is also helpful to try and find a balance when it comes to (self)evaluation. Okay, a circus artist made a mistake during their performance. Of course, that can be disappointing, but it happens. Was there anything positive you can still take out of this performance? Were there other things that went well? Perhaps the circus artist used the mistake as an opportunity to improvise or managed to make the audience believe the mistake was part of the act? Make sure these positives also get attention, this can reduce worries associated with perfectionistic concern.

Apart from the two types of perfectionism, there are three ways in which circus artists may experience perfectionism (Smith et al., 2021). The first is self-oriented perfectionism, which relates to people's self-evaluations of their own accomplishments. This way of experiencing perfectionism is how perfectionism has been approached in this chapter so far. The second way of experiencing perfectionism is socially prescribed perfectionism, which describes the pressures circus artists experience to be perfect that are imposed by others. Socially prescribed perfectionism can be caused by parents, loved ones, cast members, crew, casting agencies, social media followers, etc. This way of experiencing perfectionism describes a young circus artist who feels that their parents are unhappy with them if they do not perform to their parents' standards. The final way of experiencing perfectionism is other-oriented perfectionism, which describes circus artists who expect others in their environment to strive towards perfection. Although relevant to all circus artists, this may become particularly problematic in circus disciplines where the performance of one artist is dependent upon the performance of another, such as in teeterboard.

Out of the three ways of experiencing perfectionism, the type that is most damaging to mental health is socially prescribed perfectionism (Smith et al., 2021). Researchers have suggested that pressures from social media may have contributed to a rise in experiences of socially prescribed perfectionism. To decrease experiences of socially prescribed perfectionism, cultural changes are necessary, which are difficult to achieve and take long periods of time to occur. But that does not mean that all hope is lost. Recent research (Jowett et al., 2021) has shown that in dance, a focus on an autonomy-supportive environment is associated with less severe experiences of socially prescribed perfectionism. Chapter 4 describes how to use self-determination theory to accomplish an autonomy-supportive circus environment.

If a circus artist's perfectionistic tendencies have a severe impact on their mental health, it is useful for them to see a licensed psychologist. Research has shown that psychologists can help reduce levels of perfectionistic concern using cognitive behavioural therapy. This type of therapy includes cognitive restructuring, assertive communication, and stress management to reduce the maladaptive aspects of perfectionism (Galloway et al., 2022).

The mental health benefits of circus for recreational artists

The previous sections of this chapter described mental health problems that are likely common among circus artists. This information is relevant for professional and recreational circus artists. But given the known positive impact of physical activity on mental health and cognitive functioning (Biddle et al. 2019), it is not a leap to think that participation in recreational circus may have an inherent positive impact on mental health.

Scientific research about the mental health benefits of participation in recreational circus is still in its infancy but shows a promising impact of circus on mental health. Notably, Neave et al. (2020) tested the impact of participation in recreational circus by allocating a group of children between the ages of 9 and 12 years to either a six-month circus skills training programme or no training programme. They found no significant differences between these groups on a range of markers of mental health, but did find that those children who participated in the circus training programme reported a significant decrease in emotional problems, while the children who did not receive the circus training did not report a decrease in emotional problems. Stevens, McGrath, and Ward (2019) took a different approach and interviewed children between the ages of 8 and 14 years who participated in recreational circus. Based on the interviews, they concluded that the children believed that circus positively influenced their well-being, supported socialisation skills, encouraged enjoyment of physical activity, and built resilience to adversity. Following this, in the same age group, McGrath and Stevens (2019) concluded that investment of one dollar in the provision of circus arts training will provide a return of seven dollars when thinking of the gains in mental (and physical) health of children. Researchers have also found that there are therapeutic benefits of participation in recreational circus for people who are experiencing mental health problems. Seymour (2012), for example, found that circus gave children with autism an increased level of self-confidence and improved the level of connection between the children and their families. When interpreting these studies together, it seems likely that participation in recreational circus may improve the mental health of children.

The benefits of circus on mental health have also been investigated in the wider social circus context. The term 'social circus' is used to describe scenarios where participation in circus does not focus on achieving a high level of artistry, but rather, where participation in circus is used as a vehicle to achieve equity and personal growth (usually among communities of disadvantaged people). Several social circus programmes exist around the globe, and research that has explored the impact of these programmes has found some promising results. It is beyond the purpose of this book to critically delve into the details of social circus. In brief, however, exploratory social circus research suggests that participation in social circus may provide people with a range of disabilities a safe and inclusive environment amongst able-bodied individuals to actively participate, to experience dignity of risk, independence, and autonomy (Thompson & Broome, 2021). Examples from noteworthy social circus programmes include the Mobile Mini Circus for Children (MMCC) in Afghanistan. This programme has helped to develop an emotional culture wherein children living in a post-conflict and an ongoing-conflict scenario can feel safe and interact as part of a community (Schmeding, 2020). Social circus programmes in Ecuador and Quebec have been shown to promote the physical and mental health of those people who participated in the programme, as well as greater levels of health equity and the social change needed to sustain this level of equity (see Spiegel et al., 2015; Spiegel & Parent, 2018). Together, these studies show that social circus may be a promising vehicle to increase well-being and equity across a diverse range of socio-cultural settings.

Summary

- Mental health problems such as emotional states of stress, anxiety, depression, and disordered eating are more common among circus artists than the general population
- Circus-specific factors such as mode of engagement (for example, professional vs. amateur) and specific circus disciplines are predictive of the mental health of circus artists
- Psychological resilience is positively related to the mental health of circus artists
- Injuries have a negative impact on the mental health of circus artists
- Circus artists' levels of perfectionism are likely high, and perfectionistic concern likely negatively impacts on circus artists' mental health
- Participation in recreational circus likely has a positive impact on mental health

References

Ardern, C. L., Taylor, N. F., Feller, J. A., & Webster, K. E. (2013). A systematic review of the psychological factors associated with returning to sport following injury. *British Journal of Sports Medicine, 47*(17), 1120–1126.
Berczik, K., Szabó, A., Griffiths, M. D., Kurimay, T., Kun, B., Urbán, R., & Demetrovics, Z. (2012). Exercise addiction: Symptoms, diagnosis, epidemiology, and etiology. *Substance Use & Misuse, 47*, 403–417.
Biddle, S. J., Ciaccioni, S., Thomas, G., & Vergeer, I. (2019). Physical activity and mental health in children and adolescents: An updated review of

reviews and an analysis of causality. *Psychology of Sport and Exercise, 42,* 146–155.

Chandran, A., Roby, P. R., Boltz, A. J., Robison, H. J., Morris, S. N., & Collins, C. L. (2021). Epidemiology of injuries in national collegiate athletic association women's gymnastics: 2014–2015 through 2018–2019. *Journal of Athletic Training, 56*(7), 688–694.

Fletcher, D., & Sarkar, M. (2012). A grounded theory of psychological resilience in Olympic champions. *Psychology of Sport and Exercise, 13,* 669–678.

Galloway, R., Watson, H., Greene, D., Shafran, R., & Egan, S. J. (2022). The efficacy of randomised controlled trials of cognitive behaviour therapy for perfectionism: A systematic review and meta-analysis. *Cognitive Behaviour Therapy, 51,* 1–15.

Ganderton, C., Rayner, A., Baradell, S., Munro, D., Watson, L., & Knowles, S. R. (2021). Experiences of student circus arts performers undertaking a shoulder rehabilitation program via telehealth consultation during the COVID-19 pandemic. *Medical Problems of Performing Artists, 36*(3), 163–175.

Garner, D. M., Olmsted, M. P., Bohr, Y., & Garfinkel, P. E. (1982). The eating attitudes test: Psychometric features and clinical correlates. *Psychological Medicine, 12,* 871–878.

Gulliver, A., Griffiths, K. M., Mackinnon, A., Batterham, P. J., & Stanimirovic, R. (2015). The mental health of Australian elite athletes. *Journal of Science and Medicine in Sport, 18*(3), 255–261.

Harmon, K. G., Drezner, J., Gammons, M., Guskiewicz, K., Halstead, M., Herring, S., ... & Roberts, W. (2013). American Medical Society for Sports Medicine position statement: Concussion in sport. *Clinical Journal of Sport Medicine, 23*(1), 1–18.

Hill, A. (Ed.). (2016). *The psychology of perfectionism in sport, dance and exercise.* New York: Routledge.

Hofsess, L. (1986). Those daring young men (and women) on the flying trapeze: Impetuous folly or calculated mastery? *The Association for the Anthropological Study of Play Newsletter, 12,* 14–17.

Hughes, N. L. (2009). Changing faces: Adaptation of highly skilled Chinese workers to a high-tech multinational corporation. *The Journal of Applied Behavioral Science, 45*(2), 212–238.

Jowett, G. E., Hill, A. P., Curran, T., Hall, H. K., & Clements, L. (2021). Perfectionism, burnout, and engagement in dance: The moderating role of autonomy support. *Sport, Exercise, and Performance Psychology, 10*(1), 133–148.

Kegelaers, J., Wylleman, P., Bunigh, A., & Oudejans, R. R. (2021). A mixed methods evaluation of a pressure training intervention to develop resilience in female basketball players. *Journal of Applied Sport Psychology, 33*(2), 151–172.

Mainwaring, L. M., & Finney, C. (2017). Psychological risk factors and outcomes of dance injury: A systematic review. *Journal of Dance Medicine & Science, 21*(3), 87–96.

McGrath, R., & Stevens, K. (2019). Forecasting the social return on investment associated with children's participation in circus-arts training on their mental health and well-being. *International Journal of the Sociology of Leisure, 2*(1), 163–193.

Ménard, J. F., & Hallé, M. (2014). Circus also needs performance psychology: Facts and realities of consulting at Cirque du Soleil. In: J. G. Cremades & L. S. Tashman (Eds.), *Becoming a sport, exercise and performance psychology professional: A global perspective* (pp. 127–134). New York: Psychology Press.

Munro, D. (2014). Injury patterns and rates amongst students at the national institute of circus arts: An observational study. *Medical Problems of Performing Artists, 29*(4), 235–240.

Neave, N., Johnson, A., Whelan, K., & McKenzie, K. (2020). The psychological benefits of circus skills training (CST) in schoolchildren. *Theatre, Dance and Performance Training, 11*(4), 488–497.

Nunes, A. C. L., Mendes, L. A., Mota, L. D. A., Lima, P. O. D. P., & Almeida, G. P. L. (2022). Training load, pain intensity, and functioning can explain injuries in dancers: A classification and regression tree (CART) Analysis. *Medical Problems of Performing Artists, 37*(2), 73–77.

Pollitt, E. E., & Hutt, K. (2021). Viewing injury in dancers from a psychological perspective – A literature review. *Journal of Dance Medicine & Science, 25*(2), 75–79.

Russell, J. A., McIntyre, L., Stewart, L., & Wang, T. (2021). Concussions in dancers and other performing artists. *Physical Medicine and Rehabilitation Clinics, 32*(1), 155–168.

Sarkar, M., & Page, A. E. (2022). Developing individual and team resilience in elite sport: Research to practice. *Journal of Sport Psychology in Action, 13*, 40–53.

Schinke, R. J., Stambulova, N. B., Si, G., & Moore, Z. (2018). International society of sport psychology position stand: Athletes' mental health, performance, and development. *International Journal of Sport and Exercise Psychology, 16*(6), 622–639.

Schmeding, A. (2020). Transforming trauma in post-conflict settings: Ethnographic evidence from a social circus project in Afghanistan. In *The Routledge Companion to Applied Performance* (pp. 248–261). New York: Routledge.

Seymour, K. D. (2012). *How circus training can enhance the well-being of autistic children and their families.* Brisbane: Griffith University.

Smith, M. M., Sherry, S. B., Ge, S. Y. J., Hewitt, P. L., Flett, G. L., & Baggley, D. L. (2021). Multidimensional perfectionism turns 30: A review of known knowns and known unknowns. *Canadian Psychology/Psychologie canadienne.* Advance online publication.

Spiegel, J. B., Breilh, M. C., Campaña, A., Marcuse, J., & Yassi, A. (2015). Social circus and health equity: Exploring the national social circus program in Ecuador. *Arts & Health, 7*(1), 65–74.

Spiegel, J. B., & Parent, S. N. (2018). Re-approaching community development through the arts: A 'critical mixed methods' study of social circus in Quebec. *Community Development Journal, 53*(4), 600–617.

Stevens, K., McGrath, R., & Ward, E. (2019). Identifying the influence of leisure-based social circus on the health and well-being of young people in Australia. *Annals of Leisure Research, 22*(3), 305–322.

Stoeber, J. (2011). The dual nature of perfectionism in sports: Relationships with emotion, motivation, and performance. *International Review of Sport and Exercise Psychology, 4*(2), 128–145.

Stubbe, J. H., Tiemens, A., Keizer-Hulsebosch, S. C., Steemers, S., van Winden, D., Buiten, M.,... & van Rijn, R. M. (2021). Prevalence of mental health complaints among performing arts students is associated with COVID-19 preventive measures. *Frontiers in Psychology, 12*, 2284.

Terry-Short, L. A., Owens, R. G., Slade, P. D., & Dewey, M. E. (1995). Positive and negative perfectionism. *Personality and Individual Differences, 18*(5), 663–668.

Thompson, B. A. D., & Broome, K. (2021). Social circus for people with disabilities: A video analysis through the lens of the MOHO. *Occupational Therapy International, 2021*, 6628482.

Trott, M., Jackson, S. E., Firth, J., Jacob, L., Grabovac, I., Mistr, A. A., Stubbs, B., & Smith, L. (2021). A comparative meta-analysis of the prevalence of exercise addiction in adults with and without indicated eating disorders. *Eating and Weight Disorders – Studies on Anorexia, Bulimia, and Obesity, 26*, 37–46.

Van Rens, F. E. C. A., Burgin, M., & Morris-Binelli, K. (2021). Implementing a pressure inurement training program to optimize cognitive appraisal, emotion regulation, and sport self-confidence in a women's state cricket team. *Journal of Applied Sport Psychology, 33*, 1–18.

Van Rens, F. E. C. A., & Filho, E. (2019). Realizing, adapting, and thriving in career transitions from gymnastics to contemporary circus arts. *Journal of Clinical Sport Psychology, 14*(2), 127–148.

Van Rens, F. E. C. A., & Filho, E. (2021). Not just clowning around: Investigating psychological mechanisms underlying accidents in a heterogeneous group of contemporary circus artists. *Psychology of Aesthetics, Creativity, and the Arts, 15*(2), 377–385.

Van Rens, F. E. C. A., & Heritage, B. (2021). Mental health of circus artists: Psychological resilience, circus factors, and demographics predict depression, anxiety, stress, and flourishing. *Psychology of Sport and Exercise, 53*, 101850.

Van Rens, F. E. C.A., Metse, A. P., & Heritage, B. (2022). Exploring the mental health of circus artists: Circus factors, psychological resilience, and demographics predict disordered eating and exercise addictions. *Psychology of Sport and Exercise, 59*, 102107.

3 Stress, mental health, and performance in circus

Understanding stress

When a person believes that environmental demands (so-called stressors) are too great for them to deal with, they experience stress. An experience of stress can be positive or negative. Positive stress is called 'eustress'. People experience eustress when they believe that their ability to deal with the stressor is only slightly exceeded, and is not seen as overwhelming. When this happens, a person usually feels challenged rather than intimidated, and they would usually feel determined to push themselves towards achieving a new goal. Negative stress is called 'distress'. Negative stress happens when a person believes that they do not have the ability to deal with the stressor, which makes a person feel overwhelmed. Usually, when people say they are feeling stressed, they mean that they are feeling distressed or anxious.

People may experience stress in different aspects of their life. This means that circus artists may be struggling with for example the demands of a high training load, a tense family situation, or tight finances. The mental and physical health of a person is impacted by the sum of all the different types of stress they experience in all of their different life domains (including their life outside of circus). As a result, it is important to take a holistic approach to understanding stress. This means that circus artists should be seen as 'whole people', who also have a life outside of circus, when it comes to looking at their levels of stress, mental health, and physical health.

The Stress Process

The Stress Process by Lazarus and Folkman (1984) is a well-established psychological model that explains why and how a stressor may or may not impact on a person's performance and mental health. The stress

DOI: 10.4324/9781003289227-4

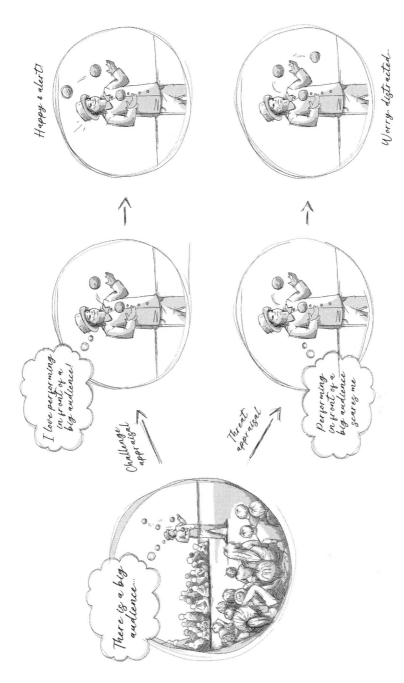

Figure 3.1 The stress process. Illustration by Sharon Krisanovski.

process starts with an environment demand, in the form of a 'stressor'. This stressor is then appraised by the circus artists. Their appraisal of the stressor will trigger the circus artist's stress response and behavioural consequences of the stressor (see Figure 3.1). The next sections describe the components of the stress process in more detail.

The stress process: stressors in circus

As previously mentioned, stressors are environmental demands experienced by a person. This means that stressors can be actual or perceived, and what may be a stressor to some might not register as a stressor by other people. For example, while one circus artist may perceive performing in a new venue as stressful, another circus artist may not give a venue change much thought at all. Stressors can occur from both physical demands (such as high training loads) and mental demands (such as high levels of responsibility for the safety of others). Both positive and negative events can be perceived as a stressor. An example of a positive stressor is getting casted to perform in a show. You may be really excited about this, but still get scared and nervous about performing in this show, wondering what it would be like to perform there, what the other cast members will be like, worry whether you are good enough, etc. An example of a common negative stressor in circus is the negative event of sustaining an injury. Stressors can be a one-off event (a so-called acute stressor) such as a last-minute adaptation to an act to make it work in a new venue. Stressors can also be chronic (long-term stressors), such as a continuous high training load. Combined, this means that there are many different types of stressors in circus. To understand these stressors better, it is useful to use a framework to categorise different types of stressors.

Research among elite athletes has identified three stressor categories that are experienced by expert performers: organisational stressors, competitive stressors, and personal stressors (Arnold, Fletcher, & Daniels, 2016; Sarkar & Fletcher, 2014). It is likely that these three types of stressors are also present in the circus industry. Organisational stressors describe demands from the environment that are caused by the organisational system in which the person operates (in this case, the circus industry). Competitive stressors are stressors directly associated with competing in sport. In circus, this would translate to performance stressors, which describe stressors that are associated with circus performance. Personal stressors refer to the experience of stressors that are not directly associated with circus. In 'The Big Mental Health of Circus Artists Survey' conducted in February of 2019 (see

Van Rens & Heritage, 2021), professional and retired professional circus artists were asked an open-ended question about the stressors they experienced in their circus careers. In total, 220 unique responses to this question were collected. These responses have not been published previously, but, for this book, each stressor that was mentioned by circus artists was categorised as an organisational, performance, or personal stressor.

Out of the three stressor categories, experiences of organisational stressors were mentioned most often. A variety of organisational stressors were reported by circus artists. The most commonly experienced organisational stressor was financial insecurity. The circus artists mentioned that this financial insecurity was caused by working as a freelance circus artist rather than having a permanent contract, the effect of injuries on pay, and the negotiation necessary to receive adequate payment for jobs. Another commonly experienced organisational stressor within circus was safety concerns. Concerns about safety ranged from concerns about the appropriateness of a venue, rigging safety, lack of appropriate/affordable training space, witnessing/learning of severe accidents of other performers, and paying jobs that were seen as inappropriate (often of sexist or sexual nature). Also, a lack of adequate health support (physical and mental) was mentioned by circus artists. Travelling circus artists in particular mentioned that it was difficult to gain access to medical personnel while on tour. Fatigue and pressure to train without adequate recovery were also seen as organisational stressors that caused health concerns among circus artists.

Several performance pressures were reported by circus artists. The harmful effects of social comparison was the most frequently reported performance stressor. More specifically, circus artists reported that their self-esteem was affected by social media posts, and that competition for jobs caused friction amongst colleagues. The circus artists explained that they felt pressured to look a certain way (thin, muscular, young) to get paying gigs, and that they felt that their bodies were sexualised and objectified in performances. Further, some circus artists reported having to perform skills for which they were not physically or mentally ready. Finally, dealing with rejections from auditions and agents was a commonly experienced performance stressor.

The most commonly mentioned personal stressor was feeling lonely and isolated. Life as a circus artist was reported to put a strain on personal relationships. The global nature of the profession – where circus artists may tour the world with a company, or travel the world by themselves chasing gigs – makes it difficult for some artists to maintain meaningful personal relationships. Feelings of isolation increased when there was a competitive and destructive culture amongst cast and crew, or poor leadership from directors/coaches. If this occurred, circus artists reported feeling alone even while being surrounded by cast and crew. On the flip side, some circus artists reported feeling lonely while off-tour because they struggled to fit into 'normal life'. Additionally, some circus artists struggled to separate their work from their identity. This is called identity foreclosure, and is a common source of stress among elite athletes in early specialisation sports such as gymnastics. Circus artists with identity foreclosure tend to suffer more when their circus careers are not going well or when they are injured, because they have not developed other identities from which they can experience feelings of self-worth.

The stress process: appraisal

Once a circus artist is aware of a stressor in their environment, the circus artist will interpret the stressor, which is called cognitive appraisal (Jones et al., 2009). What this means is that the circus artist will interpret the demand of the stressor in relation to the resources they have available to deal with the stressor. For example, the circus artist may wonder 'how is this stressor going to affect me', 'is this stressor a big deal', or 'can I cope with this stressor'. The circus artist may feel that the stressor is something they can deal with, by, for example, thinking 'this ankle sprain is a set-back, but if I work together with my physiotherapist I will be back on stage in no-time'. This is an example of challenge appraisal. However, another circus artist may think 'this ankle sprain is a big problem, I will miss out on gigs and may not be able to book new gigs once I have healed', which is an example of threat appraisal. Reappraisal is yet another type of appraisal that circus artists may use in response to a stressor, and occurs before a person's emotional response to a stressor (McRae, Ciesielski, & Gross, 2012). For example, a juggler may drop a ball (potential stressor), but may not be too concerned about this mistake, because they know how to sell this as part of their act. The way how a stressor is appraised will affect the stress response of the circus artist. Broadly speaking, reappraisal and challenge appraisal are related to better performance and mental health outcomes compared to threat appraisal (Dunne et al., 2019; Jones et al., 2009).

With help of (sport) psychologists, the way how people appraise stressors can be changed by training cognitive appraisal strategies (see Rumbold, Fletcher, & Daniels, 2012; Van Rens, Burgin, & Morris-Binelli 2021). Within the circus industry, an excellent starting point to train an artist's cognitive appraisal skills is by having them trial their tricks, acts, and shows in a low-pressure environment, prior to performing in higher-pressure environments. A low-pressure environment could include extra safety measures, a small and supportive audience, etc. The circus artist's stress response to performing in the low-pressure environment is then observed (preferably by a sport psychologist), and if the artist copes well with the stressors in the low-pressure environment, the amount of pressure in the environment can be slightly increased. If the artist does not cope well with the stressor in the low-pressure environment, the psychologist can work on mental skills with the artist to improve their cognitive appraisal prior to performing the same skill in a similar low-pressure environment again.

The stress process: stress response and behavioural consequences

The stress response of a circus artist is their physical and psychological response to the stressor. Ideally, a stressor causes an artist to feel excited and alert, and ready to perform to the best of their abilities. However, unwanted stress responses that decrease psychological well-being, such as (performance) anxiety, are also common in the performing arts (Clegg & Clements, 2022). Anxiety responses can be physical and mental. Physical anxiety responses to stressors (also known as somatic anxiety) include trembling, excessive sweating, a narrowing of the visual field, increased heart rate, increased muscle tension, feeling dizzy, feeling nauseous, vomiting, and experiencing gastrointestinal problems. All of these physical stress responses may negatively impact on performance. For example, a circus artist who is experiencing excessively sweaty hands as a result of a stress response may be more likely than usual to slip off an apparatus, while an acrobat who is experiencing higher levels of muscle tension than usual may be more likely to miss their landing after doing a trick. Examples of common mental responses (also known as cognitive anxiety) to a stressor are an inability to concentrate, excessive worrying, and breaking a previous automatic skill down in little pieces. Mental anxiety responses to stressors can also negatively impact on performance. It could for example lead to an artist seemingly forgetting their well-trained act, crying on stage, or an artist not being able to execute a skill because their excessive thinking causes de-automatisation of a previously automatic skill. Although cognitive and somatic anxiety are separate constructs, they are related to each other.

The stress response of a circus artist can also be affected by suppression, which is an active effort by a circus artist to change a response after the emotional response has happened (Gross, 2001). For example, a circus artist may feel frustrated after dropping a ball in a juggling act, and may choose to mask these feelings so that the audience is not aware of them. Research shows that suppression can cause a decrease in performance (Wagstaff, 2014) and is associated with a poorer stress response after exposure to the stressor. To optimise a stress response, it is useful to teach a circus artist reappraisal strategies, so that instead of masking feelings of frustration, the circus artist can use their response comfortably in their act. To help manage experiences of distress and anxiety, it can be useful to teach arousal-regulation strategies to circus artists. These are further explained in Chapter 9.

Balancing stress and recovery in circus

As described at the start of this chapter, it is important to realise that stress can emerge from all aspects of a circus artist's life (from circus and beyond), and that stressors can be both physical and mental. Experiences of stress are not necessarily always bad. When done right, a high training load can make a person physically stronger, as long as the person knows how to recover from this physical exertion. Similarly, experiences of mental stressors can make a person more psychologically resilient, as long as they have the time, skills, and resources to manage the stressor and to recover.

In order to avoid negative consequences of stress, it is important that stress and recovery are well balanced. This means that both physiological and psychological recovery should be an integral part of a circus artist's training plan. The scissors model by Kallus and Kelmann (2000) explains how stress and recovery should be balanced. At its core, the scissors model explains that with increasing stress, increased recovery must occur. Now imagine a circus artist who balances the usual stress in their life quite well with recovery. But then a new stressor emerges, the house the circus artist is renting has been sold, and the artist has to move. According to the scissors model, the additional stress of moving will require the circus artist to engage in more recovery than usual in order to prevent negative consequences to mental and physical health. What tends to happen though, is that people feel unable to find the time for appropriate recovery when they are overwhelmed by stress. This imbalance is likely to lead to negative mental and physical health consequences.

Ideally, circus artists actively plan moments of physiological and psychological recovery in their schedules. Building on the example of the circus artist who has to move house, this circus artist could actively schedule an extra hour of recovery time each day, in which they do not engage in strenuous mental or physical activities. What this recovery time looks like will vary from person to person based on their personal preferences. Not every recovery activity has the same effect of recuperation for all circus artists. Broadly speaking, recovery methods can be divided up into two categories: passive and active recovery. Passive recovery refers to taking rest (and pretty much means doing 'nothing'), while active recovery refers to doing something with the purpose to recover. Some active recovery strategies that may be beneficial are moving your thoughts away from the problem by, for example, watching a movie, clearing your mind by going for a walk or hanging out with friends, getting a massage, going to a flotation tank, having a warm cup of tea, etc. A circus artist may also choose to engage in purposeful arousal-regulation strategies to recover (see Chapter 9). If increasing recovery is not possible, it is also an option to decrease stress. In the example of the circus artist who has to move, a solution could be to temporarily decrease their circus-training load. In doing so, the circus artist would aim to decrease the training stress to such a level so that the combined stress of training and moving house does not exceed their coping resources. Alternatively, the circus artist may choose to reduce stress by asking a friend to help them move. This can also decrease the stress associated with the new stressor of moving.

Summary

- To understand the level of stress a circus artist experiences, it is important to consider all aspects of their lives
- There are three stressor categories: organisational, performance, and personal stressors
- The stress process explains that the way a stressor is appraised impacts a circus artist's stress response and the behavioural consequences of the stressor
- Cognitive appraisal is a mental skill that can improve with practice
- Balancing stress and recovery requires circus artists to increase recovery when stress increases

References

Arnold, R., Fletcher, D., & Daniels, K. (2016). Demographic differences in sport performers' experiences of organizational stressors. *Scandinavian Journal of Medicine & Science in Sports, 26*(3), 348–358.

Clegg, H., & Clements, L. (2022). From the wings to the stage and beyond: Performance anxiety and flow in UK vocational dance students. *Journal of Dance Education.* Advance online publication. https://doi.org/10.1080/1529 0824.2021.2004604.

Dunne, S., Chib, V. S., Berleant, J., & O'Doherty, J. P. (2019). Reappraisal of incentives ameliorates choking under pressure and is correlated with changes in the neural representations of incentives. *Social Cognitive and Affective Neuroscience, 14*(1), 13–22.

Jones, M., Meijen, C., McCarthy, P. J., & Sheffield, D. (2009). A theory of challenge and threat states in athletes. *International Review of Sport and Exercise Psychology, 2*(2), 161–180.

Kallus, K. W., & Kellmann, M. (2000). Burnout in athletes and coaches. In: Y. L. Hanin (Ed.), *Emotions in sport* (pp. 209–230). Champaign, IL: Human Kinetics.

Lazarus, R. S., & Folkman, S. (1984). *Stress, appraisal, and coping.* New York: Springer.

McRae, K., Ciesielski, B., & Gross, J. J. (2012). Unpacking cognitive reappraisal: Goals, tactics, and outcomes. *Emotion,* 12(2), 250–255.

Rumbold, J. L., Fletcher, D., & Daniels, K. (2012). A systematic review of stress management interventions with sport performers. *Sport, Exercise, and Performance Psychology, 1*(3), 173–193.

Sarkar, M., & Fletcher, D. (2014). Psychological resilience in sport performers: A review of stressors and protective factors. *Journal of Sports Sciences, 32,* 1419–1434.

Van Rens, F. E. C. A., Burgin, M., & Morris-Binelli, K. (2021). Implementing a pressure inurement training program to optimize cognitive appraisal, emotion regulation, and sport self-confidence in a women's state cricket team. *Journal of Applied Sport Psychology, 33,* 1–18.

Van Rens, F. E. C. A., & Heritage, B. (2021). Mental health of circus artists: Psychological resilience, circus factors, and demographics predict depression, anxiety, stress, and flourishing. *Psychology of Sport and Exercise, 53,* 101850.

Wagstaff, C. R. D. (2014). Emotion regulation and sport performance. *Journal of Sport and Exercise Psychology, 36*(4), 401–412.

Section 2

Optimising the circus environment to facilitate thriving

4 Engaging circus students

Understanding motivation

Once a person decides to participate in circus, it is important to understand what motivates them to engage in circus. Very broadly speaking, the term motivation describes the types of situations a person seeks out (for example, a circus class), and the amount of effort a person puts into the activity (for example, how much effort a person puts in during the class). Motivation should be seen as an interaction between personal factors (such as personality, interests, values, and goals) and the environment (such as the coach's teaching style, attractiveness of the facilities, and community spirit). This means that there is no such thing as being born as a 'motivated' or 'unmotivated' person, and that there is no such thing as a situation being motivating to every single human being. Because circus artists' personal factors are difficult to change, this chapter will mainly focus on environmental factors that are helpful to circus artists' motivation. To fully understand the impact of environmental factors on motivation, it is important to understand the different types of motivation that exist.

Distinguishing between amotivation, extrinsic motivation, and intrinsic motivation is a useful way to understand how different types of motivation impact on how people behave and perform (Deci & Ryan, 1985). Amotivation describes a person who has no motivation for an activity. A person who is amotivated towards circus is not likely to start circus, and if they start circus, they are likely to drop out. Amotivation is seen as the 'lowest' form of motivation because it usually means that people will not continue with the activity for a long time. Extrinsic motivation refers to motivation that comes from outside the person. Examples include a person participating in circus to please other people (such as parents) to win a trophy, to make money, or to look more attractive. People who are extrinsically motivated thus do not participate in circus for the sake of circus, but more so for the benefits

DOI: 10.4324/9781003289227-6

associated with doing circus. Extrinsic motivation can be useful for participation in circus, especially when a person has just started circus. But to increase the chances that a person engages in circus in the long run, intrinsic forms of motivation are important. Intrinsic motivation is the 'highest' form of motivation, and describes motivation that comes from within the person. A common example of intrinsic motivation for circus is: 'because it is fun'. Of course, it is possible for circus artists to experience different types of motivation at the same time. For example, a circus artist may do circus because it is their source of income (extrinsic) and because they think it is fun to do (intrinsic). That said, intrinsic motivation is the type of motivation that will help circus artists stay engaged in circus for many years. It is the type of motivation you will want to have among circus artists to create a positive class and cast culture, and that will ultimately help circus artists perform to the best of their abilities while being more likely to maintain high levels of psychological well-being. Therefore, circus schools and companies should be encouraged to set up the circus environment in a way that promotes experiences of intrinsic motivation among circus artists.

Nurturing intrinsic motivation using self-determination theory

Self-determination theory (Deci & Ryan, 2008) describes that people are more likely to experience intrinsic motivation when three key psychological needs are fulfilled. These three key psychological needs are a need for autonomy, relatedness, and competence (see Figure 4.1). Autonomy relates to having a sense of choice and ownership over the activity. Autonomy is the strongest predictor of intrinsic motivation, if a person's need for autonomy is fulfilled, a person is more likely to experience intrinsic motivation. Relatedness refers to whether people feel like they belong. The more relatedness a person experiences, the more likely they are to experience intrinsic motivation. Finally, competence refers to a person's perception that they are able to do the activity and that they are good at the activity. The more competent a person feels, the more likely a person is to experience intrinsic motivation. Research has shown that there are many benefits to fulfilling people's self-determined needs. Small positive changes in physical and psychological health measures are present among people who have been part of an intervention aimed at increasing the levels to which their self-determined needs are fulfilled (Ntoumanis et al., 2021). When the needs for autonomy, relatedness, and competence are fulfilled, people are better able to adhere to exercise programmes and to maintain new behaviours (Teixeira et al., 2012). Also, experiences of autonomy, relatedness,

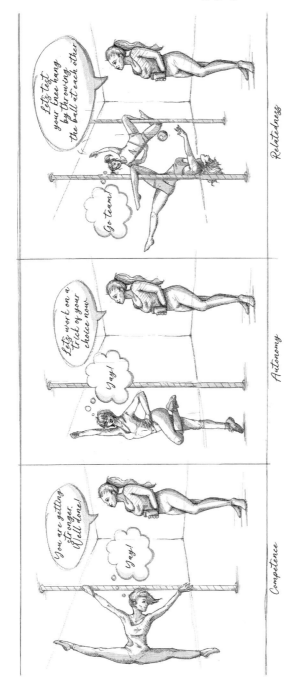

Figure 4.1 Examples of competence, autonomy, and relatedness in circus. Illustration by Sharon Krisanovski.

and competence were associated with higher levels of positive emotions, and lower levels of negative emotions in dancers (Quested & Duda, 2010). Fulfilment of these three key psychological needs has also been related to higher levels of moral behaviour and less anti-social behaviour (Ntoumanis & Standage, 2009). This means that fulfilling these psychological needs can support experiences of thriving under the big top. For this reason, it is important to consider how psychological needs for autonomy, relatedness, and competence can be fulfilled in the circus industry.

Fulfilling the need for autonomy in circus

Autonomy is argued to be the most important component of self-determination theory, because it predicts intrinsic motivation and a person's ability to stick with new behaviours best. To give circus artists' experiences of autonomy, it is important to make sure they have a voice and choice. Of course, safety is paramount, so you would not let a beginner aerialist try a difficult trick they saw on Instagram just because they want to do the trick. Instead, there are ways to structure sessions that allow even beginner students to make a few choices, thus giving them a chance to experience autonomy. For example, during warm-up, you might show the students two ways to warm up a specific part of their bodies, and then ask them to choose which option they would like to do today. This strategy will not only increase circus students' sense of autonomy but also give them a better understanding about ways to warm up their bodies. Similarly, you can remind the students of two things they worked on in the previous sessions, and let them choose individually which one they would like to work on for the next couple of minutes. This will help consolidate learning, as well as fulfil their sense of autonomy. Providing only a few options to beginner circus artists is useful, because offering too many choices can be overwhelming. This means that you would, for example, let students choose between two options (I've been thinking about our music for today, are we in the mood for Disney classics or a 1990s flash-back?), and you would avoid offering infinite options (What music are we in the mood for today?).

For intermediate and above level circus artists, the amount of options available can slowly be increased. For example, 'freestyle time' can be used to let intermediate and advanced students work on skills, transitions, and expressiveness. You might, for example, select a song (or let students choose one, prepare one, etc.) and then give students a challenge. Perhaps there is a certain skill or transition that they will need to incorporate, maybe an aerialist needs to spend at least half of the time doing floorwork, or perhaps the challenge is to express the emotion of the song. This will provide students with a sense of autonomy, but also provides structure and a goal. Letting intermediate and above circus artists set their own goals can be another excellent way to achieve a sense of autonomy. After setting these goals, you can create a plan with the students to achieve these goals, and make sure there is training time available to do work towards these goals. This might include specific drills (strength, flexibility) to achieve a goal, or might include providing progressions for the student. It is important that the circus artist is aware that these drills or progressions are likely to help them achieve their goal. For more information about setting goals, take a look at Chapter 7. For professional circus artists, and injured circus artists in rehabilitation programmes, the same principles with regard to fulfilling their need for autonomy apply. Giving circus artists a say in what their act will look like, and tailoring circus artists' rehabilitation programmes towards their own goals can be a very efficient strategy to keep the circus artist intrinsically motivated and engaged.

Fulfilling the need for relatedness in circus

Most circus training centres, schools, and companies are tight-knit communities. This shows that the circus industry is very good at creating a sense of belonging and relatedness. That said, there is always room for improvement. So yes, there are still plenty of things the circus industry can do to continue to be a community where a wide variety of people can feel accepted as they are, can make friends, and feel like they belong. The most challenging component of relatedness is making sure that beginner students experience relatedness. The circus can be an intimidating space, people are trying to do things that students may have never seen before. If an aspiring circus artist works up the courage to give circus a go, but feels intimated when they enter a circus school, the chances of that student returning for the next session are low. One important thing you can do for these beginner students is to make sure they are starting a class where others are at a similar level. For example, a 35-year-old who is trying their first ever circus class might not have done a cartwheel in about 20 years. It would be intimidating for them to be in a tumbling class with students who are doing cartwheels for warm-up and then move on to double-back flips. Of course, it is not always possible for every circus school to have enough students to cater for classes tailored towards the level of the circus artists, but catering for different levels can make a massive difference in the retention rate of a circus school. Scheduling a series of 'introduction to circus' classes for aspiring students is another useful step to make sure that beginners are not scared off by advanced students.

To make yourself relatable, it is also important to introduce yourself to new students or cast members. This introduction should go beyond simply saying your name and what your circus speciality is. Tell new circus students/cast members about something else that you love. Perhaps you are obsessed with baking, or maybe you make bandanas for your dog. Adding something like that to the mix will make you less of an unrelatable circus-superstar, and more of a human in the eyes of a new, aspiring circus artist. When a new student/cast member enters a pre-existing class/cast, also make sure you introduce this person to another person in the group. For example, walk with the new circus artist to an existing group member and say something along the lines of the example presented in Textbox 4.1.

TEXTBOX 4.1 Example of an introduction

Hi Fatma, this is [new person], they are trying circus for the very first time today. Fatma has been doing circus with us for a few months now, and she has the most adorable cat. Fatma, can you team up with [new person] today?

Being introduced like this will give the new person a chance to learn one person's name (rather than having to learn many in one go, and then forgetting all of them). Mentioning something about Fatma, such as how long she has been training circus, and the fact that she has a cat, also gives the new student some easy topics to talk about. Chances are Fatma and the new person will start chatting about how Fatma got into circus and what her cat is like. Finally, asking Fatma to team up with the new person will make Fatma feel responsible to include the new person in the group.

Doing team exercises can also be an excellent tool to create relatedness. But be mindful that not everybody enjoys having strangers in their personal space (in fact, this can scare people off for several reasons). For example, an attempt at partner juggling is definitely something you could try to build relatedness because this does not require people to enter others' personal space. Some partner stretches, on the other hand, where one partner may sit on top of the other, does require an intrusion of one's personal space, and is something that is not always appropriate. These types of exercises can be a bit much for people, especially when they do not know others in the group very well. Giving people options, and a sense of autonomy for exercises that require others in their personal space is a good idea to prevent circus artists from feeling overwhelmed (this includes asking for consent; see Chapter 5). It should probably go without saying, but the same goes for spotting of circus artists who are learning new tricks.

Once students have attended some of your circus classes, it becomes important to show them that you are a community. To start small, try to make an effort to not just learn students' names, but also to use them (for example, say 'great work Miguel!' instead of 'great work!'). If you are set on creating a strong sense of community, you might also want to consider hosting events. Perhaps this is a circus-related movie night in your studio, or maybe there is a circus in town and some instructors go to the show together with students. Perhaps students are interested in learning more about things relevant to circus, and you arrange workshops about theatre skills, first aid, mental health first aid, stage make-up, costume design, etc. with experts in these areas. Some of these experts might be instructors or students at your circus school, others might be external to your circus school. I would recommend you to choose something that matches with the identity of your circus school. For example, if your focus is fitness, fitness-related workshops may be more appropriate, while if your focus is creativity, creative workshops are probably more relevant to your clients.

You might even want to consider creating apparel or other items with the logo of your circus school to increase relatedness among circus students or cast. Of course you could choose to sell this apparel, but you also consider giving students a merchandise item upon completion of the first series of classes (#team circus), or after they have been selected to perform in a show. Imagine how nice it would be to see your students proudly wearing a T-shirt with your logo on it! If your circus school is bigger, you might even want to consider apparel or other forms of merchandise based on discipline (for example: [name school] team unicycle). You could even create special items for students who joined a showcase ([circus school] 2023 showcase performer). Coaches/instructors might wear a shirt with the circus school's logo and the word 'instructor' on it to show their affiliation with the school. If you decide to create apparel, make sure it is accessible to all students. This means that you will need to be size-inclusive to achieve the effect of relatedness if you decide to opt for apparel. If this is not feasible, then it might be best to think of other options (socks, notebooks, re-usable water bottles, etc.).

Finally, to be relatable, it is important that you have a clear vision about who your target audience is. Once you have established this, make sure you represent this target audience to the best of your abilities. For example, if you want your school to be accessible to people of all fitness levels, and your marketing material only shows images of people with shredded bodies doing crazy tricks, it is unlikely that you will attract people with lower fitness levels. Similarly, if your marketing material only consists of images of Caucasian females, you will be less likely to attract people who do not identify as female, or who are not Caucasian. To achieve high levels of relatedness for your target audience, it is thus important that your marketing material is an accurate representation of your target audience. At the same time, you want to make sure that you are not misrepresenting who your current circus students and instructors are. This means that showing that half of your student population in an aerial silks class is male in your marketing material, but in actuality having no male aerial silks students is not useful. A male may sign up for your classes, but they would be more likely to drop out if they expected to see other males in the class. This also means that in an ideal world, your staff represents the diversity of your target audience.

Fulfilling the need for competence in circus

To fulfil a circus artist's need for competence, it is important that they see progress, receive encouragement, and feel like they are good at what they do. The simplest form to help fulfil a person's need for competence is providing positive feedback. This can be non-verbal feedback (such as a smile, applause, or a high five) or verbal feedback (such as saying, 'well done Jason', 'great work Mustafa', or 'yes Damian, work it!'). Positive feedback is even more powerful when it is tailored towards the individual. So, although there is nothing wrong with giving a high five, or saying 'good job today Sarah', it is even more effective to say to a student 'you have been working very hard on that trick over the past few weeks, and I can see your hard work is paying off Sarah, you are so close to getting it!'. This does not only acknowledge their progress and effort, but also shows your awareness of their goals.

A strength of the above example is that the feedback does not just focus on skills. Some skills are difficult for students to acquire, and some students make progress more quickly than others. By acknowledging other things than physical skill acquisition, such as teamwork, effort, determination, and artistic expression, you give students a wide range of areas that they can feel competent in, that are all important in the circus industry. If progress in one area is not going as fast as the artist would like (for example, flexibility), the circus artist still has plenty of opportunities to feel competent, for example, because they are strong, and are continuously improving their character work.

This also means that there is nothing wrong with complimenting an artist on the striking pattern on the fun leggings they might be wearing.

After all, wearing exciting leggings is a type of artistic expression. That said, it is best to take focus away from what circus artists' bodies look like (for example, do not compliment a person on how muscular their legs look in those fun leggings). You can find more information on this in Chapter 5. This also means that when you notice a student is getting stronger, it is best to compliment them based on how strong they have become (Noah, did you just set a personal best for your pull-ups? You are getting so strong!) rather than how strong people look (Wow Noah, look at those shoulder muscles popping out when you are doing your pull-ups!).

Finally, when you provide positive feedback to a circus artist, it is important that you base this on something they can control. A compliment like 'you are so talented Maria' can be quite frustrating for a circus artist. Yes, they might be talented, but talent is not the only reason why they are such a great circus artist. The hard work, determination, and setbacks they dealt with go unacknowledged in a compliment about talent. It is much more valuable to let a circus artist know that you are impressed by what they can do, and the work they must have put in to becoming such a great circus artist. By acknowledging this, you increase the chances that the circus artist experiences a feeling of competence.

How a circus artist's attributions affect motivation

Even when a circus artist is in an environment where they receive positive feedback, this does not always mean that a circus artist feels competent. The reasons why a person believes they were successful, or why they believed they failed also impact on their feeling of competence. The explanations people give as to why they believe they were successful or unsuccessful in something are called attributions (see Rees, Ingledew & Hardy, 2005). Generally speaking, people's attributions of their successes and failures can be analysed on five different dimensions. The first dimension is whether the cause is internal or external to the person. The second dimension is whether the cause is seen as within or outside of their control. The third dimension is whether the cause is seen as stable or unstable over time. The fourth dimension describes whether the cause is seen as global, and relating to all the situations the person faces in their life, or whether it is seen as specific to this situation. Finally, the fifth dimension is universality, whether the cause is unique to the person or the same for everybody in the world. For example, a circus artist might think, 'I managed to do this new trick today, because I have been working so hard on it'. Hard work is something that is internal to the person (it is something they do), it is something that is within their control (they can choose not the work hard), it is unstable (next time they can choose not work hard), it may be seen as global (because hard work may pay off in a range of different situations), and it could be seen as universal (everybody who works hard will accomplish this trick). Attributions like the one in this example are generally motivating to circus artists, because it encourages them to continue to work hard to achieve success in circus and beyond. An example of an attribution for success that is generally not good for motivation is, 'I managed to do this new trick today, because I got lucky'. Luck is generally perceived as a factor outside of the person (it is not something you do that makes you lucky), that is not in their control (you cannot control your level of luck), it is unstable (next time you might get unlucky), it may be seen as global (luck causes success in a range of different situations), and it could be seen as not universal (some people are more lucky than others). As a result, luck is unlikely to motivate a person to continue to work hard to achieve success. If a circus artist believes they are successful only due to dumb luck, they may even start to feel helpless.

Attributions can also be made for failure, and these are even more important to understand. If a circus artist believes that: 'I am still not getting the splits because I am just not a flexible person', they have made an internal, outside of their control, stable attribution, that is not global, and not universal. An attribution like this shows that the circus artist believes that they are unlikely to ever get the splits – or that they need to do much more work than others to achieve success – because they believe their bodies simply cannot do it. As a result, they are likely to feel discouraged to continue to work on their splits, and for this reason, they are unlikely to get their splits and experience success. On the contrary, a circus artist who believes that: 'I am still not getting the splits because I need to set aside more time to work on my flexibility', has made an internal, in their control, unstable attribution, that could be seen as global and universal. An attribution like this one shows that the person believes they could eventually get the splits if they dedicate enough time to it. As a result, they might decide to continue plodding along on training their flexibility, and for this reason, they are more likely to get their splits.

If you are coaching circus artists who tend to make unhelpful attributions (such as, 'I am just not a strong person', 'I just got lucky', 'the only reason I can do this is because my coach is great'), it is important to give the circus artist a helpful attribution in the feedback you provide to them. Imagine Tom just did a new trick for the first time, and you know Tom is going to attribute his success to something external to him, such as his fantastic coach. In this case, you can help Tom's motivation by saying, 'Nice work on getting that trick Tom, your dedication to getting stronger is really paying off!'. By saying this, you give Tom a helpful internal, controllable, unstable attribution. This will make it more likely that Tom will feel competent, increasing the chances of him experiencing intrinsic motivation, and thus increasing chances that he will continue to do circus.

Summary

- There are different types of motivation, such as intrinsic, extrinsic, and amotivation
- Intrinsic motivation is important for people to continue with circus in the long run
- Creating experiences of autonomy, relatedness, and competence will likely increase circus artists' experiences of intrinsic motivation and well-being
- Experiences of autonomy can be created by giving circus artists choices
- Experiences of relatedness can be created by giving circus artists a sense of belonging via, for example, teamwork and team attire
- Experiences of competence can be created by providing circus artists with positive feedback for goal accomplishments
- The way how circus artists explain their successes and failures impacts on the amount of competence they experience
- Internal, controllable, unstable, global, and universal attributions for success are generally beneficial to the motivation of circus artists

References

Deci, E. L., & Ryan, R. M. (1985). Cognitive evaluation theory. In *Intrinsic motivation and self-determination in human behavior* (pp. 43–85). Boston, MA: Springer.

Deci, E. L., & Ryan, R. M. (2008). Self-determination theory: A macrotheory of human motivation, development, and health. *Canadian Psychology/Psychologie Canadienne, 49*(3), 182.

Ntoumanis, N., Ng, J. Y., Prestwich, A., Quested, E., Hancox, J. E., Thøgersen-Ntoumani, C.,... & Williams, G. C. (2021). A meta-analysis of self-determination theory-informed intervention studies in the health domain: Effects on motivation, health behavior, physical, and psychological health. *Health Psychology Review, 15*(2), 214–244.

Ntoumanis, N., & Standage, M. (2009). Morality in sport: A self-determination theory perspective. *Journal of Applied Sport Psychology, 21*(4), 365–380.

Quested, E., & Duda, J. L. (2010). Exploring the social-environmental determinants of well-and ill-being in dancers: A test of basic needs theory. *Journal of Sport and Exercise Psychology, 32*(1), 39–60.

Rees, T., Ingledew, D. K., & Hardy, L. (2005). Attribution in sport psychology: Seeking congruence between theory, research and practice. *Psychology of Sport and Exercise, 6*(2), 189–204.

Teixeira, P. J., Carraça, E. V., Markland, D., Silva, M. N., & Ryan, R. M. (2012). Exercise, physical activity, and self-determination theory: A systematic review. *International Journal of Behavioral Nutrition and Physical Activity, 9*(1), 1–30.

5 Creating a circus environment that nurtures psychological well-being

Nurturing self-confidence in circus artists

The term self-confidence (sometimes called self-efficacy) is used to describe the extent to which a person believes they are going to be successful (Vealey, 1986). There is an optimal level of self-confidence for the well-being and performance of circus artist. Having too low levels of self-confidence is harmful to circus artists, because low levels of self-confidence are related to lower levels of performance (Woodman et al., 2010; Woodman & Hardy, 2003) and higher levels of burnout (Kjøormo & Halvari, 2002). Being overconfident, on the other hand, can also be detrimental to circus artists, because it may decrease the effort they put into performing, and as a result their performance levels may drop too (Woodman et al., 2010). For example, Nina is a cyr wheel artist with an optimal level of self-confidence. She thinks her act is challenging, but also believes she will be successful and perform it well. As a result, Nina is more likely to experience high levels of psychological well-being, and to perform her act well. Georgia, on the other hand, has low levels of self-confidence. She believes her cyr wheel act is too challenging for her, and she fears she will not perform it well. As a result, she is more likely to make mistakes, and to experience lower levels of psychological well-being. Finally, Jasmine is overconfident. She believes her cyr wheel act is boring and much too easy for her. She believes that the performance of her act requires no effort, and as a result she may not try very hard to do her best work. This means that it is unlikely that she performs to the best of her abilities.

Some people generally feel more self-confident than others; this describes the 'trait' component of self-confidence. That said, the situation a person is in can also impact their levels of self-confidence. This describes the 'state' component of self-confidence. For example, a circus artist may generally feel quite self-confident as a performer (trait

DOI: 10.4324/9781003289227-7

self-confidence). Now, imagine this circus artist is performing two different disciplines in a show. This artist may feel very confident about their cyr wheel act, but a little bit less confident about their straps act (state self-confidence). In general, doing exercise or physical activity increases people's levels of self-confidence. Recreational participation in pole dancing, for example, has been related to increases in people's levels of self-confidence and body acceptance (LePage & Crowther, 2010; Nicholas et al., 2019). This means that, broadly speaking, participation in circus has the potential to be good for people's levels of self-confidence.

To understand how to nurture the self-confidence of circus artists, it is important to understand how people develop levels of self-confidence. Bandura (1977) describes that there are four key factors that impact the development of self-confidence. The first, and most important one, is a person's past performance. People who have experienced success in the past are more likely to believe that they are going to be successful in the future. For example, a cyr wheel artist who was successful in the progressions leading up to a rock start to waltz is likely to feel confident about their ability to successfully do the rock start to waltz. Negative experiences on the other hand, such as experiences of failure, will decrease the self-esteem of a circus artist. For example, a cyr wheel artist who failed to achieve many tricks in the past will likely not feel very confident about their ability to successfully do the rock start to waltz. To nurture the self-confidence of circus artists, it is thus important to make sure that artists have many opportunities to experience success in circus. One way to achieve this is by teaching skills that are appropriate to the level of the circus artist, so that the artists can experience success each step of the way towards achieving a skill. This is particularly important for vulnerable circus students with low levels of self-esteem, and those who have experienced failure in the past (such as people who feel like they are 'bad' at physical activity because they had unpleasant experiences during physical education classes in school).

The second factor that impacts on the self-confidence of circus artists is vicarious experiences. The term 'vicarious experiences' describes the impact that watching other people achieve success can have on a person. For example, if a circus artist wants to learn a new skill, and sees an artist who they believe to be similar to them successfully achieve the skill, their levels of self-confidence will likely increase just by observing the circus artist being successful. The circus artist will likely think, 'if they can do it, I can do it!'. If the circus artist sees a similar artist fail at a skill, this will likely negatively impact the self-esteem of the circus artist, because the circus artist may think 'if they cannot do it, I will probably not be able to do it either'. To nurture the self-esteem of circus artists, it is thus important to make sure that they see artists they can relate to succeed. Role models can thus also play a role in the vicarious experiences of circus artists. Role models can be anybody a circus artist relates to, such as coaches, parents, colleagues, (older) siblings, friends, and the list goes on. One efficient way to facilitate the self-esteem of teenaged circus students is to invite a successful past student to the school to have a chat about their road to success.

The third factor that impacts on the self-confidence of circus artists is (verbal) persuasion, which involves the encouragement and discouragement circus artists receive. An example of using verbal persuasion to nurture the self-confidence of a circus artist is to tell a young circus artist that you believe they could have a great future as an artist if they continue to work hard. Although verbal persuasion impacts on the self-confidence of circus artists of any age, encouragement is especially important for young circus artists, such as children and teenagers. Discouragement, such as telling circus artists that you do not believe they 'have what it takes' to become successful under the big top, will likely negatively impact the self-confidence of the circus artist.

The fourth and final factor that impacts the self-confidence of circus artists is their physiological state. This describes the circus artists' level of psychological and physiological well-being in a specific situation. Let us compare two examples. Toby had a couple of great jumps with their partner on the teeterboard, they are feeling strong, their favourite coach tells them that they are ready to try their first double back on the board, and their trusted catcher is ready to help them. Toby will likely feel quite self-confident about attempting this skill. Manu, on the other hand, had a few jumps with his partner on the teeterboard that felt a bit out of synch; he is feeling a bit tired and does not trust his catcher fully. If Manu's coach tells him that he is ready to attempt his first double back on the board, Manu will likely feel less self-confident than Toby.

In summary, the self-confidence of circus artists can be nurtured by making sure that they have plenty of opportunities to experience success while doing circus, by encouraging the use of role models the students can relate to, by providing positive feedback, and by making sure that circus artists are in an environment that puts them into a positive physiological state.

Body objectification in circus

Body objectification describes the extent to which a person believes that their body is an object that is evaluated (Fredrickson & Roberts,

1997). For example, a circus artist in a burlesque show may believe that they will be judged negatively by the audience if their body is not lean and muscular. Research has shown that a person who is experiencing high levels of body objectification is more likely to engage in disordered eating, experience symptoms of depression, have lower levels of body esteem, and lower levels of self-esteem, (Hebl, King, & Lin, 2004; Strelan, Mehaffey, & Tiggemann, 2003; Tiggemann & Kuring, 2004). The reason for this is that high levels of body objectification are related to experiences of body shame and appearance anxiety (Tiggemann, 2013). Circus artists are more likely to engage in disordered eating than the general population (Van Rens, Metse & Heritage, 2022; see also Chapter 2). It is thus likely that circus artists experience high levels of body objectification.

Research among people who participate in fitness has shown that several factors can impact on the level of body objectification a person experiences while exercising. Some of these factors are internal to the person. An important internal factor is the reason why the person chooses to participate in physical activity. If a person engages in exercise to change their weight or appearance, they are likely to experience lower levels of body satisfaction, body esteem, and self-esteem (Strelan, Mehaffey, & Tiggemann, 2003). If a person engages in exercise for functional reasons (such as getting stronger), this has a positive impact on body satisfaction, body esteem, and self-esteem. It is likely that self-objectification and appearance-related reasons to engage in circus have a similar impact on the well-being of circus artists. Apart from this internal factor, several external factors, such as clothing, mirrors, and social media use, could also impact on the level of body objectification circus artists experience.

Clothing and body objectification in circus

Although no research has specifically looked at the impact of circus costumes on well-being, it is likely that the clothing worn by circus artists – be it during training or during performance – impacts on circus artists' levels of body objectification and psychological well-being. Uniforms in cheerleading, for example, have been found to impact on eating disorder risk and body image. Midriff revealing uniforms in particular were found to have a negative impact on the well-being of the cheerleaders wearing the uniform (Torres-McGehee et al., 2012). Alarmingly, the negative impact of wearing skimpy outfits on body objectification has been found to persist even after the person has changed into their regular clothes (Quinn, Kallen, & Cathey, 2006).

Levels of body dissatisfaction and the risk of eating disorders and disordered eating are particularly high during teenaged years and early adulthood. It is no surprise then, that teenaged girls in particular report high levels of discomfort with their sports uniforms (Lauer et al., 2018).

There are differences between circus disciplines in terms of their clothing requirements. Physical safety is a critical feature of clothing in a range of circus disciplines. For example, a Chinese pole artist will likely experience many burns if they do not wear jeans and a sweater, while an aerial silks artist is in danger of getting stuck in the silks if they were to wear trackpants and a baggy T-shirt while training. When considering the impact of clothing on the physical safety of circus artists, it is also important to consider their psychological safety. Research has identified differences in the prevalence of disordered eating between circus disciplines (Van Rens, Metse, & Heritage, 2022). It is possible that clothing and costume choices play a role in this. From this perspective, circus schools, training centres, and companies should be encouraged to critically assess the costumes selected for any shows, starting with the costumes for the most vulnerable groups: teenagers, young adults, and beginner circus artists. Questions to ask yourself are: what costumes are you currently using?, how are decisions for costume choices made?, do the artists have a say in this process? And, if you are mostly using skimpy clothing, what safe alternatives could be appropriate for the circus discipline? Recently, the German Gymnastics Federation decided to take action after reflecting on their female gymnasts' experiences with body objectification and sexualisation in response to the leotards that are normally worn by athletes in this sport. At the Tokyo 2020 Olympics, the German woman's gymnastics team members wore beautiful full-length unitards. It may be appropriate for some circus disciplines to follow suit, and change the attire of their artists to include a broader range of options.

Aside from assessing costume choices for performance purposes, it is also worth reflecting on the attire-culture during circus training. When looking around your circus training centre, what do people tend to wear? Do people mostly were crop tops, muscle tops, or go shirtless? Then allow yourself to critically assess why this may occur. Again, differences between disciplines are to be expected for practical reasons. In dance pole, for example, there is a clear advantage to wearing as little as possible to stick to a chrome, powder-coated, stainless steel, or brass pole. That said, would sticky leggings be something that could be beneficial to some of your students? Similarly, it is worth carefully weighing the pros and cons of silicone-covered poles. Critically thinking about this will help you assess to what extent body objectification is happening in your circus school or company. Reflecting on this can be quite difficult and confronting. It may even make you think about your own relationship with your body. If you feel like it is time to make a change, you may choose to lead by example. For instance, if you believe sticky leggings would stand out in your pole studio, but you feel comfortable enough to give them a go, then you may decide to wear them the next time you are going to train.

One good practice example related to clothing is from a coach called Vee (not her real name). Vee has a six-pack that could go on the front cover of any women's fitness magazine without the use of photoshop. During a class for advanced students, Vee was wearing leggings and a sports bra. Understandable, given how hot it was in the training space. After teaching this class, Vee was getting ready for the next class that was aimed at beginners. In preparation for this class, Vee put on a baggy T-shirt, which she nonchalantly tucked into her full-length leggings. Surprised, I asked her why she did this. She said she observed that her beginner students were at times intimidated by her physique, claiming that they would not be able to do skills she was showing them because they did not have the abs to do them, and apologising to her about their weight when she was physically spotting tricks. She noticed this happened less when she was wearing more clothes. Consequently, she decided to start wearing a baggy T-shirt in all beginner classes. This example clearly shows that by paying attention to her students' behaviour, Vee had figured out a way to decrease body objectification among beginner circus students. Similarly, some circus training spaces have set rules for all coaching staff to wear a full-length top whenever there are recreational students in the venue. This will also help prevent body objectification among vulnerable circus students.

Body objectification and social media

Clothing choices during training sessions can help fight body objectification in circus, but there is more that can be done. Social media are another space where objectification is rampant (Bell, Cassarly, & Dunbar, 2018). Body objectification and sexualisation of circus on social media may get you gigs, likes, and followers. But from a psychological well-being perspective, it is worth reflecting on how you use your body in your social media posts. Of course, being comfortable with your body is great, and this is not to say that bodies must be hidden from social media. Instead, it is worth reflecting on the messages your posts are sending. Questions you may ask yourself are: what am I wearing in my circus-related social media posts?, do I use filters or apps to make images more flattering?, how may my posts impact the self-esteem of my followers?, and what is the reason why I post what I post? From a psychological perspective, ideally, a social media account shows variety. This gives followers the opportunity to see that there are all sorts of different ways how you can engage in circus. Another way to decrease body objectification of circus artists on social media is to consider how you respond to posts from others. A question you may ask yourself is: do you 'like' images of circus artists regardless of what they wear? For example, do you 'like' videos of pole dancers training in their track pants? Also, when commenting on a post, do you focus on how incredible it is what the person is doing (for example: 'you make that difficult skill look effortless!'), instead of commenting on what their body looks like? If the answer to these questions is 'yes', you are contributing to a decrease in body objectification in circus on social media.

Mirrors and body objectification in circus

Aside from what people wear, the layout of a circus space can also contribute to a psychologically safe circus space. One thing to consider is the role of mirrors when it comes to the psychological safety of vulnerable circus artists (such as beginners and teenagers). From a purely psychological perspective, there is some evidence that large mirrors could negatively impact the well-being of vulnerable students (Hausenblas, Brewer, & Van Raalte, 2004). Research has shown that the presence of large mirrors can cause a heightened awareness of one's physique during yoga and exercise classes (Frayeh & Lewis, 2018; Martin Ginis, Burke, & Gauvin, 2007). As a result, mirrors can increase self-presentational concerns of people who are already worried about their physique (such as people with high levels of social physique anxiety, women, teenagers, and beginners). This in turn can lead to decreased enjoyment of physical activity. Importantly, Radell, Adame, and Cole (2004) conducted a study that looked at the impact of the presence of mirrors in a beginner ballet course. Their findings showed that students who took the course in a room where there were mirrors present had lower levels of body satisfaction, and achieved less progress on a range of skills upon completion of the course compared to students who took the course in a room without mirrors. However, Raedeke, Focht, and Scales (2007) nuanced that it may not just be the presence of mirrors that may have a negative impact on body satisfaction and exercise enjoyment. They found that, whether there are mirrors in the room or not, students in an exercise class enjoyed the class more when the coach focused on health benefits as opposed to improvements in physique. Although at this stage it is difficult to provide clear advice on the best use of mirrors in circus, it might be worth investing in curtains or blinds that can be used to hide mirrors when teaching more vulnerable groups of circus students (such as beginners, teenagers, and young adults). At the same time, it is important that coaches focus on changes in the functional ability of their students, rather than changes in their looks.

Coaching circus to nurture well-being

There is currently no formal universal pathway towards becoming a circus coach or trainer. Although some certified circus coaching courses exist for a range of circus disciplines, most of these courses focus on how to teach circus in a physically safe way (for example, by going over different physical spotting techniques). Very few (if any) circus coaching courses train the skills required to create a circus climate that nurtures the psychological well-being of artists. This means that many circus coaches are flying blind when it comes to developing their coaching and leadership styles, with most of them learning by trial and error.

In sport, transformational leadership has become a popular leadership style used to improve performance, self-confidence, and team cohesion (Arthur, Bastardoz, & Eklund, 2017). The core goal of transformational leadership is to empower others, and transformational leaders try to avoid controlling their followers. To achieve this, transformational leaders implement four behaviours (Bass & Reggio, 2006). The first is idealised influence, which means that transformational leaders practise what they preach, lead by example, and serve as role models. For instance, a transformational leader would not tell a group of circus artists to work together for an act. Instead, the transformational leader works together with circus artists to make sure they collaborate in their act. The second transformational leadership behaviour is inspirational motivation, which involves the leader communicating a clear vision of what they believe is possible to achieve. The transformational leader delivers this vision in an optimistic and inspiring way, which makes circus artists believe that more is possible than they initially thought. The third behaviour is intellectual stimulation. A transformational leader does not do the thinking for circus artists. Instead, a transformational leader asks questions and challenges circus artists to think for themselves. This means that circus artists become an active part of decision-making processes. Intellectual stimulation will help circus artists feel more confident in their abilities. Finally, transformational leaders engage in individualised consideration. They display empathy and try to understand the individual needs and abilities of each circus artist (and crew member) they work with. After learning about these needs and abilities, a transformational leader tries to fulfil these needs and makes use of the circus artist's capabilities.

Consent in circus

A final important – and challenging – aspect to consider in relation to creating a circus environment that nurtures well-being and psychological safety is the matter of consent. Consent refers to a person voluntarily doing something, or a person voluntarily allowing a person to do something. This means that the term consent can be used for a range of matters relevant to the circus industry. An artist can consent to their picture being taken, to wear a particular costume, to mentor another artist, to be touched (for example, as part of physical spotting or a partner act), to do a trick out of safety lines, etc. Encouragingly, explicitly asking for consent seems to be common practice in the circus industry, and tends to be seen as a display of good manners. For example, most circus students ask their coaches whether they can film them doing a trick.

Most discussions about consent in circus involve topics that are potentially triggering for a circus artist. From observations, it seems that consent to touch is a particularly important topic of discussion in the circus industry. In many circus disciplines, touch is useful at times. Touch can be used to speed up the learning process, to ensure the circus artist is engaging the correct muscles, to correct a circus artist's posture/lines, to increase a stretch, to keep an artist safe, and some circus disciplines such as adagio would simply not exist without the involvement of physical touch. As a consequence, many discussions take place in the circus industry regarding the importance of asking for consent to touch, and how to ask for consent. Asking for consent is very important, and as previously mentioned does not just relate to consent for touch. Asking for consent is not related to the gender of the artist or coach, any circus artist should be asked for consent.

When done right, asking for consent can empower all parties involved. For example, coach Jenna asked student Christopher for consent to physically spot him while he attempts a trick. Christopher consents to this. Christopher will likely feel empowered because he has been given autonomy when he was asked for consent. Jenna may feel empowered because she can now fully focus on her job to keep Christopher safe, because she knows Christopher has given consent to be physically spotted in case things go awry. The question how to ask for consent then remains. The answer to this question is complex. Table 5.1 lists the do's and don'ts of asking for consent.

A crucial factor to consider when asking for consent is whether you are asking for global consent or specific consent. Requests for specific consent are about specific situations, such as, 'Jess, are you happy for me to push you a little bit deeper into your split-stretch today?'. Global consent is about consent for less specific matters, such as 'Jess are you okay with me touching you to help you improve your skills during class?'. Global requests for consent can be a great starting point to get a broad understanding of a circus artist, and if deemed crucial to the circus discipline, some global consent requests may even be part of a safety waiver that circus artists sign. That said, asking for specific consent can empower a circus artist further. A good practice example regarding specific consent comes from a clowning class. During this class, students were learning a technique used to make the audience believe that one clown slapped the other in the face, without actually striking the clown. This technique required

Table 5.1 Do's and don'ts of asking for consent

Do	Don't
Ask every circus artist for consent, regardless of their gender	Assume a person's consent
Ask explicitly for consent	Assume that consent in one situation translates to consent in another situation
Ask for situation-specific consent	Punish people for not giving consent
Consider the impact of any unequal or dependent relationships	Judge people for not giving consent
Consider the age of the person who is being asked to provide consent (particularly minors)	Push people to explain why they are not giving consent (but listen if they volunteer to explain their reasons)
Listen to the response to the request for consent, and behave in accordance with the response	
Provide context to your request	
Ask for individual consent	
Consider cultural differences	

one clown to make a striking movement towards the other clown's face. Students formed groups of two, and were instructed to explicitly ask each other whether they were happy to practise this skill. If the answer to this question was yes, they then asked whether the clown on the receiving end of the strike was ready, prior to making the striking movement. The clowns then continued to ask each other whether they were happy to practise the skill again each time before they made an attempt. This gave the students an easy opportunity to stop practising the skill in case they started to feel uncomfortable. Another good practice example related to stretching was a circus school that designed thick, laminated, cards that had a different print on each side. One side of the card indicated that the student was happy to be touched during the stretch, while the other side indicated that the student preferred not to be touched during the stretch. The purpose of the cards was explained to each new student at the circus school. When the stretching component of training commenced, all circus artists grabbed a card, and for each stretch, they would use the card to indicate whether they were happy to be touched during the stretch or not. This method of asking for consent is empowering to circus artists because they did not have to give consent in front of a group of people (for example, other students), they did not have to provide a reason, and they could change their mind dependent on the stretch they were doing. For coaches, this method is useful because it removes any sense of doubt.

It is also important to consider the type of relationship between the person who is asking for consent and the person who is asked for consent. If this is a dependent (for example, circus artist – casting director) or an unequal (for example, circus artist – coach) relationship, asking for consent can be quite difficult. For example, if a circus artist knows that the person who is asking for consent is their casting director, and the casting director will make the decision whether or not they will be part of the cast of a show, the circus artist may not feel that their consent is voluntary. They may feel forced to give consent, because they may believe there are negative consequences to saying 'no'. For this reason, if a circus artist is in an unequal or dependent relationship, it is important to provide them with context why they are being asked for consent. A best practice example comes from Joey (not his real name). At the start of his class, Joey introduced himself to the group of students he was about to coach. He first mentioned that he was excited to teach new skills, and that he would support the students' development using progressions, but that he was happy to physically spot any students if they felt more comfortable attempting a skill that way. After this, Joey said that it was important to him that all of his students were safe. He explained that mistakes happen. And then, he said that if he saw something going wrong, and it looked like a student would get hurt, he would try his best to intervene by grabbing any body part within reach to ensure the safety of the student. He then asked the students if they were okay with this approach. All of the students responded with a 'yes'. There are many strengths to this example. Firstly, being open about your role in the specific circus environment can make people feel at ease. Secondly, Joey provided context to his request by explaining that safety was extremely important to him. Thirdly, he non-judgmentally provided options to the students in terms of how they prefer to learn (either with touch or without). Finally, he explicitly asked for consent. This means that he asked people to say 'yes', rather than taking the absence of a 'no' as consent. One way Joey could have improved his method of asking for consent is by asking all students individually whether they consented, as opposed to asking his students as a group.

Further, it is good practice to consider a person's age and cultural background when asking for consent. When working with minors, it is useful to ask for consent of parents first (for example, 'If Cheng is okay with it, can I gently push him further into his stretch to help him increase his flexibility?'). If the parent does not consent, then listen and do not push the child into his stretch. If the parent consents, then ask for consent from the child (for example, 'Cheng, are you okay with me gently pushing you deeper into this stretch?'). If the child does not consent, then listen and do not push the child further into the stretch. Cultural background is also important to consider, because some things that are seen as 'normal' in some cultures, are less common in others. Touch is a clear example of this. In some countries, such as Greece, Spain, India, Turkey, and France, touch is much more common in daily life compared to other parts of the world, such as the United States, Canada, Northern Europe, and Australia. For example, a Spanish circus coach working in New York may have a strong inclination to help their students using physical touch, and may forget to ask for consent simply because physical touch is a natural thing to do in their culture. The Spanish coach may then genuinely feel confused to hear that they made their American students feel uncomfortable. For this reason, it is important to reflect on your culture, and how this may impact on your behaviour in circus. This awareness can guide you towards appropriate levels of asking for consent in a range of different situations.

Summary

- Self-confidence describes a person's perception whether they are going to be successful
- Four factors impact on the development of self-confidence, the most important one is past experiences
- Recreational participation in circus likely has a positive impact on self-esteem
- Body objectification describes the extent to which a person believes their body is an object that is judged
- High levels of body objectification can have a negative impact on well-being in circus
- The clothing and costumes used in circus can impact body objectification
- Social media should be used wisely, to decrease body objectification in the circus industry
- Mirrors could increase levels of body objectification among vulnerable circus artists
- Adopting a transformational leadership style nurtures the well-being of circus artists
- Asking for voluntary consent is important, and it is good practice to ask for situation-specific consent

References

Arthur, C. A., Bastardoz, N., & Eklund, R. (2017). Transformational leadership in sport: Current status and future directions. *Current Opinion in Psychology, 16,* 78–83.

Bandura, A. (1977). Self-efficacy: Toward a unifying theory of behavioral change. *Psychological Review, 84*(2), 191–215.

Bass, B. M., & Reggio, R. E. (2006). *Transformational leadership* (2nd ed.). Mahwah, NJ: Lawrence Erlbaum Associated, Inc.

Bell, B. T., Cassarly, J. A., & Dunbar, L. (2018). Selfie-objectification: Self-objectification and positive feedback ("likes") are associated with frequency of posting sexually objectifying self-images on social media. *Body Image, 26,* 83–89.

Frayeh, A. L., & Lewis, B. A. (2018). The effect of mirrors on women's state body image responses to yoga. *Psychology of Sport and Exercise, 35,* 47–54.

Fredrickson, B. L., & Roberts, T. A. (1997). Objectification theory: Toward understanding women's lived experiences and mental health risks. *Psychology of Women Quarterly, 21,* 173–206.

Hausenblas, H. A., Brewer, B. W., & Van Raalte, J. L. (2004). Self-presentation and exercise. *Journal of Applied Sport Psychology, 16*(1), 3–18.

Hebl, M. R., King, E. B., & Lin, J. (2004). The swimsuit becomes us all: Ethnicity, gender, and vulnerability to self-objectification. *Personality and Social Psychology Bulletin, 30*(10), 1322–1331.

Kjøormo, O., & Halvari, H. (2002). Relation of burnout with lack of time for being with significant others, role conflict, cohesion, and self-confidence among Norwegian Olympic athletes. *Perceptual and Motor Skills, 94*(3), 795–804.

Lauer, E. E., Zakrajsek, R. A., Fisher, L. A., Bejar, M. P., McCowan, T., Martin, S. B., & Vosloo, J. (2018). NCAA DII female student-athletes' perceptions of their sport uniforms and body image. *Journal of Sport Behavior, 41*(1), 40–63.

LePage, M. L., & Crowther, J. H. (2010). The effects of exercise on body satisfaction and affect. *Body Image, 7*(2), 124–130.

Martin Ginis, K. A., Burke, S. M., & Gauvin, L. (2007). Exercising with others exacerbates the negative effects of mirrored environments on sedentary women's feeling states. *Psychology and Health, 22*(8), 945–962.

Nicholas, J. C., McDonald, K. A., Peeling, P., Jackson, B., Dimmock, J. A., Alderson, J. A., & Donnelly, C. J. (2019). Pole dancing for fitness: The physiological and metabolic demand of a 60-minute class. *The Journal of Strength & Conditioning Research, 33*(10), 2704–2710.

Quinn, D. M., Kallen, R. W., & Cathey, C. (2006). Body on my mind: The lingering effect of state self-objectification. *Sex Roles, 55*(11–12), 869–874.

Radell, S. A., Adame, D. D., & Cole, S. P. (2004). The impact of mirrors on body image and classroom performance in female college ballet dancers. *Journal of Dance Medicine & Science, 8*(2), 47–52.

Raedeke, T. D., Focht, B. C., & Scales, D. (2007). Social environmental factors and psychological responses to acute exercise for socially physique anxious females. *Psychology of Sport and Exercise, 8*(4), 463–476.

Strelan, P., Mehaffey, S. J., & Tiggemann, M. (2003). Brief report: Self-objectification and esteem in young women: The mediating role of reasons for exercise. *Sex Roles, 48*(1), 89–95.

Tiggemann, M. (2013). Objectification theory: Of relevance for eating disorder researchers and clinicians?. *Clinical Psychologist, 17*(2), 35–45.

Tiggemann, M., & Kuring, J. K. (2004). The role of body objectification in disordered eating and depressed mood. *British Journal of Clinical Psychology, 43*(3), 299–311.

Torres-McGehee, T. M., Monsma, E. V., Dompier, T. P., & Washburn, S. A. (2012). Eating disorder risk and the role of clothing in collegiate cheerleaders' body images. *Journal of Athletic Training, 47*(5), 541–548.

Van Rens, F. E. C.A., Metse, A. P., & Heritage, B. (2022). Exploring the mental health of circus artists: Circus factors, psychological resilience, and demographics predict disordered eating and exercise addictions. *Psychology of Sport and Exercise, 59*, 102107.

Vealey, R. S. (1986). Conceptualization of sport-confidence and competitive orientation: Preliminary investigation and instrument development. *Journal of Sport and Exercise Psychology, 8*(3), 221–246.

Woodman, T., Akehurst, S., Hardy, L., & Beattie, S. (2010). Self-confidence and performance: A little self-doubt helps. *Psychology of Sport and Exercise, 11*(6), 467–470.

Woodman, T., & Hardy, L. (2003). The relative impact of cognitive anxiety and self-confidence upon sport performance: A meta-analysis. *Journal of Sports Sciences, 21*(6), 443–457.

6 Sustainable talent development in circus

Understanding talent development

Many different talent development pathways may lead to a professional career as a circus artist. Some common pathways include growing up in a circus family, transitioning to circus from (elite) sport, transitioning to circus from another performing arts form, and completing a bachelor's degree in circus arts after recreational engagement in circus. For most circus companies, these different pathways mean that they employ a cast with quite diverse strengths and weaknesses. For example, a former gymnast who joins a circus company will usually have extraordinarily well-developed physical skills, but might have less developed artistic skills compared to a circus artist who grew up in a traditional circus family. To make sure that their future cast has developed the skills they require, some circus companies such as Cirque du Soleil have chosen to create their own development programmes to teach circus artists the performance skills that they find important (Van Rens & Filho, 2019). This chapter outlines key features of a circus talent development pathway that contributes to thriving under the big top.

Achieving a professional performance career in circus is not an easy feat. Aspiring circus artists need to dedicate many hours towards training their artistic, physical, and mental skills. Effective talent development is important to guide and support aspiring circus artists in their journey towards a career under the big top. Talent development is a popular topic, many books have been written about what it takes to become an expert or elite performer. Unfortunately, there is quite a bit of misinformation published about talent development. One of the most common myths about talent development is the so-called '10,000 hour rule' (Ericsson & Smith, 1991), which is widely interpreted to mean that 'anyone can become an expert at a skill if they practise the

DOI: 10.4324/9781003289227-8

skill purposefully for a total of 10,000 hours'. The truth is that training circus for 10,000 hours does not make a professional circus artist, because the training quality is just as important as the training quantity. Repeating a skill over and over again is going to help make a skill automatic, but simple repetition is unlikely to lead to an expert level of performance (Ericsson & Pool, 2016). Research in circus confirms this. Circus training methods that are based on repetition and rigid progressions were found to produce large performance gains in the short term, but in the long term, this method disengages circus artists and causes performance plateaus where artists' skill levels increase until a point where they do not improve any further (see Burrt & Lavers, 2017).

Instead, purposeful practice is suggested to be more effective in developing talent than repetition. Purposeful practice includes components of self-assessment such as setting goals (see Chapter 7) and monitoring one's progress towards these goals. It also requires circus artists to focus fully on the activity during training, it includes receiving feedback, and pushes a circus artist to challenge oneself and continuously develop further (Ericsson & Pool, 2016). The type of practice believed to be most efficient in developing talent is called 'deliberate practice'. According to Ericsson and Poole (2016), deliberate practice includes the elements of purposeful practice that have just been described, as well as the guidance of an expert coach who can design practice activities to help the artist continuously improve their performance. This means that a high level of expertise is required from coaches to help circus artists reach increasingly higher levels of performance, and that coaches need to adopt a transformational leadership style to facilitate decision-making by circus artists (see Chapter 5).

The importance of holistic talent development

'Holistic talent development' is key to sustainable talent development in performance domains such as circus, dance, and sport. Holistic talent development describes a focus on the development of a person as a whole, rather than solely focusing on the development of circus skills (Henriksen & Stambulova, 2017). Holistic talent development thus provides opportunities for an aspiring circus artist to develop their physical, cognitive, and psycho-social skills, which will prepare them for thriving under the big top and beyond. The reason why holistic talent development is so important is three-fold. First, the reality is that not all aspiring circus artists will make it to a full-time professional performance career. Despite their efforts, some will not achieve a professional circus performance career at all, while many others combine their performance career with other roles in circus (such as coaching) or beyond (a career outside of circus). Second, many circus disciplines are physically taxing: injuries and ageing could contribute to a relatively early retirement from circus. This means that even those who do achieve a professional circus career may have to think of a second career after their circus career ends. Finally, holistic talent development can help protect the mental health of circus artists when they experience setbacks during their circus careers.

Research in sport overwhelmingly shows that holistic talent development allows a person to see themselves as more than an athlete and develop identities beyond sport (Stambulova & Wylleman, 2014). A circus artist who has reaped the benefits from holistic talent development may, for example, see themselves as a circus artist, parent, a friend, and information technology (IT) specialist. To be able to form these multiple identities, it is important that a circus artist has the opportunity to explore other roles, and the opportunity to choose which roles they would like to fulfil (Van Rens, Ashley, & Steele, 2019). For example, to form an identity as an IT specialist, it is important that the circus artist finds IT interesting, and that they have the time and resources to develop their IT skills. Having multiple strong identities is an indicator of higher levels of mental health, such as lower levels of substance use, lower levels of burnout, and less issues upon retirement in athletes (Brewer & Petitpas, 2017). This is likely the same for circus artists. For example, a circus artist who solely depends on their circus identity may think: 'I have nothing now that I cannot seem to book any gigs'. A circus artist with multiple strong identities may experience this situation differently, and may think: 'I do not have many gigs coming up, I will use this time to stay up to date with the newest IT developments'. For sustainable talent development in circus, it is thus important to give artists the opportunity to explore, develop, and maintain other life domains that they find valuable.

At the moment, very little is known about the identity development of circus artists. It is unclear whether circus artists generally have multiple strong identities. It is also unknown how the pathway that has led to a professional circus career impacts circus artists' overall sense of self. In some early specialisation sports, such as gymnastics, research has shown that talent development systems generally do not support the holistic development of a person (Lavallee & Robinson, 2007). This may mean that circus artists who once were gymnasts may not have had the opportunity to develop multiple identities, which could lead to lower levels of mental health compared to other circus artists. There is some evidence that indicates that there may be a more holistic focus on talent development in circus compared to gymnastics. In the words of a circus artist: 'Gymnasts pretty much only develop the body, and their mind stays almost in a box. So now [in circus] we were totally developing our minds, our bodies, and our souls' (Van Rens & Filho, 2019).

The lifespan model (Wylleman & Lavallee, 2004) proposes that holistic talent development needs to be developmentally appropriate. This means that holistic talent development looks different based on the age of the circus artist. For circus artists under the age of 18, it is important to promote the opportunity to complete a high-school qualification, and to facilitate contact with peers, siblings, parents, and coaches. This may be challenging to achieve in some circus pathways, for example, those growing up on stage touring with circus families. For circus artists aged 18–25, relationships with the artists' partners and coaches are of increased importance from a psycho-social perspective, while higher education and other forms of vocational training and experience become important from a vocational developmental perspective. Again, this may be challenging to achieve in some circus talent development pathways. For example, if a circus artist attends a national circus school to obtain a bachelor's degree in circus arts, this may negatively impact holistic talent development, because the aspiring artist's vocational development is fully centred around circus. For sustainable talent development in circus, it is thus useful to consider how each individual pathway may impact the artists' ability to holistically develop themselves, as opposed to looking solely at the development of their circus-specific skills. That said, more research is needed to understand the impact of talent development in circus on the well-being of circus artists.

Skills transfer in circus talent development

This brings us to the importance of skills transfer for the purpose of holistic talent development in circus. Transferrable skills are skills that are learned in one domain (such as circus) but can also be used in other domains. For example, a circus artist may learn how to take care of their body, how to make decisions under pressure, how to come up with creative solutions for problems, and how to effectively communicate to connect with an audience. Although these skills are generally seen as central to thriving in a circus career, these skills can also be central to thriving in life domains outside of circus. It is useful for circus artists to learn how they can use these skills to their advantage outside of the big top.

To maximise the likelihood that circus artists are able to use their skills outside of the big top, it is important to consider how skills are taught (Billing, 2007). First, it is important to provide practical examples when teaching skills that may be transferred to other settings and to couple these examples with actions. For instance, when teaching a circus artist to connect to an audience, it is important to not only teach them about the theory of body language, but to also explain some actions they may want to do (such as using gestures while talking). After this theory, it is important to give them the opportunity to practise these actions (in this example, physically practise using body language). Secondly, it is important to teach skills in a social setting. In the example of connecting with an audience, it is thus important to make sure the circus artist can practise this skill with others, rather than by themselves. Thirdly, it is important for skill transfer to give circus artists the opportunity to explore how they can use these skills outside of the circus. A relatively simple way to accomplish this is to ask circus artists questions along the lines of 'in what other scenarios can you use these skills?'. Based on their responses, you may then do a practice session. For example, a circus artist may say that the newly learned communication skills could also be useful when teaching circus students. They can then practise this skill in a different setting using a role-play scenario. Finally, it is important that circus artists learn how to monitor their own use of these transferrable skills, and how effectively they believe they used the skill. This can be accomplished by teaching circus artists how to use journaling techniques for reflective purposes.

Developing mental health literacy in circus

Given the low levels of mental health in circus (see Chapter 2), mental health literacy can be crucial to thriving under the big top. For this reason, developing mental health literacy should be an important component of talent development in circus. It is also useful for others in the circus industry (such as coaches, physiotherapists, directors, etc.) to have high levels of mental health literacy. The term 'mental health literacy' describes a person's understanding of how to achieve and maintain high levels of mental health, their understanding of mental illnesses and their treatments, their ability to effectively seek help, and low levels of stigma related to mental illnesses (Kutcher, Bagnell, & Wei, 2015; Kutcher, Wei, & Coniglio, 2016). This book can be used to increase circus-specific mental health literacy. That said, complementary approaches can be used to solidify mental health literacy among those in the circus industry.

Completing an accredited 'Mental Health First Aid' course is one approach that has been proven to be effective in increasing people's abilities to recognise mental illnesses, to change beliefs about treatment of mental illnesses, to increase confidence in providing help to people with mental illnesses, to increase helping behaviour, and to decrease social distance from people with mental illnesses (Hadlaczky et al., 2014; Kitchener & Jorm, 2002). In a nutshell, Mental Health First Aid courses are similar to the well-known physical first aid courses, except that they cover issues related to mental health. The courses are based on scientific evidence and have been designed to empower and equip people with the knowledge, skills, and confidence to support a friend, family member, or co-worker who is experiencing a mental health problem. Mental Health First Aid courses are delivered by accredited mental health professionals who facilitate group discussions in a safe space. After successfully passing an exam, people who complete this course will receive a certificate. To date, accredited Mental Health First Aid courses exist in 24 countries, including Australia, Canada, France, Hong Kong, Japan, Malaysia, India, Saudi Arabia, the United Kingdom, and the United States. You can find more information about these courses on https://mhfainternational. org. Mental Health First Aid courses are thus accessible in many parts of the world and could be an excellent step towards increasing mental health literacy in the circus community. Completion of this course can help circus artists take care of themselves and others, and it can also empower circus coaches, physiotherapists, directors, and other crew. As described in Chapter 2, many circus artists find it difficult to receive mental health support while touring. Having certified Mental Health First Aiders as part of the cast and crew of travelling circus shows could be an important step towards improving mental health under the big top.

Mental skills training for circus artists

Mental skills training describes the systematic practice of mental skills with the ultimate goal to increase thriving (Weinberg & Gould, 2019). Although there is little research about the impact of mental skills training on circus artists, research from sports, other performing arts, and medicine has shown that mental skills training is useful to pretty much all performers (see, for example, Birrer & Morgan, 2010; Clark & Williamon, 2011; Stefanidis et al., 2017). Both beginners and professionals can benefit from training their mental skills, and mental skills can be useful for people who are experiencing problems, as well as those who are not experiencing problems (Weinberg & Gould, 2019). Despite the overwhelming evidence on the usefulness of mental skills training, such training is often not integrated into talent development because many people do not really understand how to practise or teach mental skills, and some people still wrongly believe that mental skills are just something a person is born with.

Just like any physical circus skills, mental skills should be trained and developed. At its core, training mental skills is quite similar to training physical circus skills. It requires consistent and repeated training, progress is monitored and self-assessed, and feedback is provided. Ideally, mental skills training would thus be a core component of training sessions, similar to how warming up, strengthening, stretching, and cooling down are core components of circus training. Also, mental skills training programmes should ideally be designed or informed by qualified experts, just like how physical skills training should be guided by qualified professionals. To achieve this, some circus schools and companies may want to contact sport or performance psychologists to develop mental skills training programmes that are relevant to their artists.

Mental skills training should thus be an integral component of talent development in circus. Section 3 of this book discusses, explains, and applies the basics of key mental skills that are useful for circus artists. These skills include goal setting and self-talk (Chapter 7), mental imagery (Chapter 8), a range of relaxation and arousal-regulation strategies such as progressive muscle relaxation, stretching, diaphragmatic breathing, mindfulness, and pre-performance routines (Chapter 9), as well as psycho-perceptual motor skills and visual anticipation (Chapter 10).

Summary

- There are currently many different pathways that lead to professional circus careers
- Simply training circus skills for 10,000 hours will not make an expert circus artist
- Using a holistic approach to circus talent development can contribute to thriving in circus
- Providing circus artists with opportunities to develop multiple identities is likely to positively impact on their mental health
- Skills that have been learned in circus can be used in other life domains if they are taught in the right way

- Mental health literacy can be a powerful contributor to thriving under the big top
- Mental skills training involves the systematic training of mental skills, and has the potential to facilitate thriving under the big top

References

Billing, D. (2007). Teaching for transfer of core/key skills in higher education: Cognitive skills. *Higher Education*, *53*(4), 483–516.

Birrer, D., & Morgan, G. (2010). Psychological skills training as a way to enhance an athlete's performance in high-intensity sports. *Scandinavian Journal of Medicine & Science in Sports*, *20*, 78–87.

Brewer, B. W., & Petitpas, A. J. (2017). Athletic identity foreclosure. *Current Opinion in Psychology*, *16*, 118–122.

Burrt, J., & Lavers, K. (2017). Re-imagining the development of circus artists for the twenty-first century. *Theatre, Dance and Performance Training*, *8*(2), 143–155.

Clark, T., & Williamon, A. (2011). Evaluation of a mental skills training program for musicians. *Journal of Applied Sport Psychology*, *23*(3), 342–359.

Ericsson, K. A., & Pool, R. (2016). *Peak: Secrets from the new science of expertise.* Boston, MA: Houghton Mifflin Harcourt.

Ericsson, K. A., & Smith, J. (Eds.) (1991). *Toward a general theory of expertise: Prospects and limits.* Cambridge: Cambridge University Press.

Hadlaczky, G., Hökby, S., Mkrtchian, A., Carli, V., & Wasserman, D. (2014). Mental health first aid is an effective public health intervention for improving knowledge, attitudes, and behaviour: A meta-analysis. *International Review of Psychiatry*, *26*(4), 467–475.

Henriksen, K., & Stambulova, N. (2017). Creating optimal environments for talent development: A holistic ecological approach. In: J. Baker, S. Cobley, & J. Schorer (Eds.), *Routledge handbook of talent identification and development in sport* (pp. 270–284). London: Routledge.

Kutcher, S., Bagnell, A., & Wei, Y. (2015). Mental health literacy in secondary schools: A Canadian approach. *Child and Adolescent Psychiatric Clinics*, *24*(2), 233–244.

Kutcher, S., Wei, Y., & Coniglio, C. (2016). Mental health literacy: Past, present, and future. *The Canadian Journal of Psychiatry*, *61*(3), 154–158.

Kitchener, B. A., & Jorm, A. F. (2002). Mental health first aid training for the public: Evaluation of effects on knowledge, attitudes and helping behavior. *BMC psychiatry*, *2*(1), 1–6.

Lavallee, D., & Robinson, H. K. (2007). In pursuit of an identity: A qualitative exploration of retirement from women's artistic gymnastics. *Psychology of Sport and Exercise*, *8*(1), 119–141.

Stambulova, N. B., & Wylleman, P. (2014). Athletes' career development and transitions. In: A. Papaioannou & D. Hackfort (Eds.), *Routledge companion to sport and exercise psychology* (pp. 605–621). London: Routledge.

Stefanidis,D.,Anton,N.E.,Howley,L.D.,Bean,E.,Yurco,A.,Pimentel,M.E.,& Davis, C. K. (2017). Effectiveness of a comprehensive mental skills curriculum in enhancing surgical performance: Results of a randomized controlled trial. *The American Journal of Surgery, 213*(2), 318–324.

Van Rens, F. E., Ashley, R. A., & Steele, A. R. (2019). Well-being and performance in dual careers: The role of academic and athletic identities. *The Sport Psychologist, 33*(1), 42–51.

Van Rens, F. E. C.A, & Filho, E. (2019). Realizing, adapting, and thriving in career transitions from gymnastics to contemporary circus arts. *Journal of Clinical Sport Psychology, 14*(2), 127–148.

Weinberg, R. S., & Gould, D. (2019). Introduction to psychological skills training. In *Foundations of sport and exercise psychology*, 7th ed. (pp. 261–284). Champaign, IL: Human Kinetics.

Wylleman, P., & Lavallee, D. (2004). A developmental perspective on transitions faced by athletes. In: M. Weiss (Ed.), *Developmental sport and exercise psychology: A lifespan perspective* (pp. 507–527). Morgantown, WV: Fitness Information Technology.

Section 3

Mental skills for thriving in circus

7 Goal setting and self-talk in circus

Goal types in goal setting

Most circus artists set goals for themselves. These goals range from statements such as 'I want to become a professional circus artist' to 'I want to be able to land my double-back somersault on the teeterboard'. When done right, goal setting can be a powerful tool to increase a circus artist's ability to adhere to their training programme, to increase their levels of performance, and to increase well-being (Weinberg, 2010). Unfortunately, few people understand goal setting well. Research from sport has shown that many athletes and coaches think about and imagine their goals, but they do not consistently write their goals down. This means that goals are often forgotten, and not prioritised. For goal setting to be at its most powerful, it is helpful for coaches and circus artists to regularly set aside some time to set goals, to write the goals down in a dedicated place, and to create action plans to achieve these goals. Further, it is useful to actively seek feedback with regard to the progress towards achieving these goals. Tracking progress made towards achieving a goal can be very motivating and can help people achieve their goals (Weinberg, 2010).

To set goals that facilitate thriving under the big top, it is important to consider the different types of goals a circus artist may set. First, it is useful to set both short-term and long-term goals. Long-term goals are broader picture end-goals, such as 'I want to become a professional circus artist'. Long-term goals can be quite daunting, and can take a long time to achieve. For this reason, short-term goals can be very useful. Because they can describe the steps the circus artist may take in order to achieve their long-term goals (Tenenbaum et al., 1991). Short-term goals can include specific tricks to learn, the progressions towards getting these tricks and so forth. Setting short-term goals can thus serve as a plan for a circus artist to achieve their long-term goal.

DOI: 10.4324/9781003289227–10

For example, the circus artist with the long-term goal to become a professional circus artist, could set short-term goals that describe when to train, what to train, and what research to do. This will help them take steps towards their long-term goals.

Secondly, goals can be categorised as approach and avoidance goals (Elliot, 1999). Approach goals are goals that state what a person wants to achieve, for example, 'I want to achieve a single arm handstand'. Avoidance goals describe what a person does not want to happen, for example, 'I do not want to be the only circus artist in the troupe who cannot do a single arm handstand'. Research from sport has shown that setting avoidance goals can decrease mental health, social relationships, and increase anxiety (Adie, Duda, & Ntoumanis, 2010; Eum & Rice, 2011; Kuster et al., 2017). For this reason, circus artists and coaches should focus on setting approach goals.

Finally, goals can be analysed based on the type of achievement they describe. The first type of achievement goals are outcome goals. Outcome goals focus on achieving a particular outcome in a specific situation. In circus, a common example of this would be to get casted for a particular show or gig. The problem with this type of goal is that achievement depends on many factors outside of the circus artist's control. For example, getting casted depends not only on how well the circus artist does during an audition, but also depends on the skills of other circus artists who may audition, any specific role requirements the circus artist may be unaware of, and the preferences of the casting director. Outcome goals can, for a short period of time, increase motivation. In the long-term, however, outcome goals are not very beneficial to thriving. Mastery goals on the other hand, describe goals that are not impacted by external sources and that are within a person's control. An example of a mastery goal is to 'achieve a 20 second hold of a single arm handstand during the audition'. Because mastery goals are not impacted by external factors, they tend to be more beneficial to people's mood and performance (Halvari, Skjesol, & Bagøien, 2011; Weinberg, 2010), especially when the goal is set by the circus artist themselves (Benita, Roth, & Deci, 2014).

When a circus artist sets a goal, it can be classified within each of the three sets of goal types described in this section. For example, the goal 'I do not want to be the first person to fall out of a handstand hold during training today' can be categorised as a short-term, avoidance, outcome goal. Psychological research has shown that the combination of mastery and avoidance goals (for example, 'Last time I held a handstand for 55 seconds during training, today I do not want to do worse') has the most negative impact on performance (Van Yperen,

Elliot, & Anseel, 2009). This was the case regardless of how difficult the person thought the goal was, personal characteristics of the participants, and the type of tasks they were completing. For this reason, it is best not to set avoidance mastery goals in circus. Instead, circus artists should be encouraged to set approach mastery goals, such as 'I am going to hold a handstand for 60 seconds during training today' (Lochbaum & Gottardy, 2015).

Effective goal setting using the SMARTS principle in circus

To create effective approach mastery goals, it is useful to follow the SMARTS principle (Weinberg & Gould, 2019). When goals are set using the SMARTS principle, people are more likely to be successful in achieving their goal compared with goals that are not based on SMARTS (Weinberg & Gould, 2019). SMARTS is an acronym, in which every letter stands for a component that helps people set effective goals.

- The first S of SMARTS stands for *Specific*. Specific goals exactly state what a person wants to achieve. An example of a specific goal is 'being able to do 10 pull-ups in a row'. Specific goals are thus very clear; there will be no confusion among circus artists in terms of what achieving '10 pull-ups' may be. An example of a non-specific version of a similar goal is to 'get stronger'. Different circus artists may interpret this goal differently, because what is 'getting stronger' really? A goal of achieving '10 pull-ups' is much clearer.
- The M of SMARTS stands for *Measurable*. Measurable goals are goals of which achievement can easily be measured. For example, achievement of the goal 'being able to do 10 pull-ups in a row' is easily measurable, because you can count how many pull-ups a circus artist is able to complete. A goal that would be much more difficult to measure would be 'getting stronger', because there is no clear indication how this will be measured. Is the circus artist required to do pull-ups, hold a plank as long as they can, or do a certain amount of crunches? The goal leaves too much room for interpretation in terms of what aspects of strength a person should improve.
- The A of SMARTS stands for the *Action* involved to achieve the goal. Action-oriented goals are goals that describe what a person should do, as opposed to solely focussing on the end destination. For example, if a beginner circus artist is unable to do 1 pull-up,

but has a goal of 'being able to do 10 pull-ups in a row', they will likely not know what to do to get to the point of being able to do ten pull-ups in a row. Instead, the goal for this student should include the type of exercises they should do, how often they should do this exercise, and how many repetitions they should do. This action-oriented approach will avoid confusion and will help them achieve the desired end result. An example of an action-oriented goal to achieving ten pull-ups in a row could be 'doing two sets of five reverse pull-ups four times per week this week'. After achieving this goal, a new action-oriented goal can be set to guide the circus artist towards the ten-pull-ups in a row.

- The R of SMARTS stands for *Realistic*. This means that the goal should be within reach of the circus artist. Based on their strengths, weaknesses, and personal resources (for example, available time to work on circus skills), different circus artists would thus ideally set different goals.

- The T of SMARTS stands for *Time-bound*. Time-bound goals are goals that indicate a time frame, so that the circus artist knows this goal does not cross an infinite timespan. An example of a time-bound goal is 'doing 30 minutes of stretching, five days per week, for one month'. The time-bound component of this example relates to the amount of days per week, and the duration during which the circus artist will work towards the goal (one month).

- The last S of SMARTS stands for *Self-determined*, which means that the goal is set by the circus artist (or at the very least, with input of the circus artist).

Setting SMARTS goals is something that might seem easy, but often goes wrong. To test your understanding of the SMARTS principle, take a look at Table 7.1. Can you determine which components of SMARTS are covered in each example? You can find the answers at the end of this chapter, after the Summary.

Table 7.1 Exercise: which components of SMARTS are covered by these goals?

1 To get the middle splits by the end of the month
2 To practise juggling four balls for ten minutes per day for one month
3 To do progressive muscle relaxation before going to sleep
4 To lose ten kilograms of weight by the end of the month
5 To improve my circus act by practising it three times per week for the next two weeks

When setting SMARTS goals, it is important to keep goal flexibility in the back of your mind. Many outside sources can impact on performance (such as sleep, injuries, life distractions, etc.). It is therefore important to adjust goals when necessary. The adjustment of goals should be seen as part of the *Realistic* aspect of SMARTS, and should not be interpreted as failure.

Understanding self-talk

In a sense, self-talk can be described as pretty much everything a person thinks (Van Raalte, Vincent, & Brewer, 2016). As a result, it includes the things a person says to themselves out loud, as well as thoughts that remain unspoken. Broadly speaking, three different types of self-talk exist (Van Raalte, Vincent, & Brewer, 2016). The first type is positive self-talk, which describes positive thoughts a person has, for example, 'training is going to be great today because I'm really looking forward to working on this new skill'. The second type of self-talk is instructional self-talk, which describes a person giving themselves instructions about, for example, skill execution, such as 'I now need to wrap the silk three times around my leg and then I need to pull myself up'. The final type of self-talk is negative self-talk, which describes a person's negative thoughts such as 'training today is going to be horrible because I have to work on this scary new trick'. In sport, the optimal use of self-talk strategies has been found to improve skill acquisition, learning, performance, and self-confidence and reduce anxiety (Hatzigeorgiadis et al., 2009, 2011). More specifically, the use of positive and instructional self-talk predicted significantly higher levels of performance and performance consistency among gymnasts, while negative self-talk was related to lower levels of attention, cognitive and emotional control, and self-confidence (Van Dyke et al., 2018) (Figure 7.1).

To maximise the gains of self-talk, it is important to practise self-talk, and to persist with it. Self-talk is usually automatic and habitual, which means that people are often not aware of the self-talk they are using. This lack of awareness makes it difficult for a person to change their self-talk. One exercise to try to figure out the proportion of positive, negative, and instructional self-talk used by a circus artist is the elastic bands experience. At the start of, for example, a training session, the circus artist will be given approximately 50 elastics bands (the office supply ones usually suffice). The circus artist will begin the training session wearing all these elastics bands on their right arm. Whenever the circus artist catches themselves using

Figure 7.1 Positive, negative, and instructional self-talk. Illustration by Sharon Krisanovski.

positive self-talk, they move one band from their right arm to their left arm. When they use negative self-talk, they move a band from their right arm to their left ankle. If they use instructional self-talk, they move a band from their right arm to their right ankle. At the end of the training session, the circus artist can analyse how often they use self-talk (that is, how many bands have moved from the right arm to another limb), and what types of self-talk they use most often (that is, which limb ended up with the most elastic bands). When doing the elastic bands exercise, of course make sure that it is safe to use in the circus discipline, and that the bands are not too tight. Once the circus artist is aware of the amount of self-talk they use, and the proportion of positive, negative, and instructional self-talk, we can analyse whether their self-talk is conducive to their motivation, self-confidence, and performance. If a circus artist uses a lot of negative self-talk, it is important to consider optimising their self-talk by reducing negative self-talk.

To reduce negative self-talk, many people will instinctively try to use the strategy of thought stoppage, which involves trying not to think the 'forbidden thought'. Research however shows that this strategy is not effective. This counterproductive process of stopping thoughts is described as an ironic effect. Researchers have found that people who were asked not to think about something (in this case a polar bear) are more likely to think about this forbidden thought (Wegner, 1989). More importantly, research from sports has also shown that forbidden thoughts are even more counterproductive when athletes are under pressure. In this research, trained athletes were asked to complete a task and obtain a desirable outcome. In some situations, athletes were also told to avoid a 'forbidden' outcome. The athletes completed this task while under pressure and while not under pressure. The researchers found that the 'forbidden' outcome occurred most often when the athletes were under pressure and were told to avoid the 'forbidden' outcome (Woodman, Barlow, & Gorgulu, 2015). Attempting to avoid 'forbidden' thoughts or outcomes is thus not a good idea, particularly when a circus artist is under pressure. Instead, thought-swapping has been shown to be an effective method to change self-talk. Thought-swapping involves replacing the negative thought with a positive or instructional one. In other words, if you do not want a circus artist to think about a polar bear, do not forbid them to think about this. Instead, ask them to think about something else, such as a penguin.

Swapping thoughts in circus

To reap the most benefits of thought-swapping, it is important to consider what alternative to the negative thought would be most useful for
the circus artist. Table 7.2 provides some suggestions on how to change
different types of negative self-talk to positive or instructional types
of self-talk.

Table 7.2 Swapping thoughts: examples

Negative self-talk	Positive self-talk	Instructional self-talk
I will never be able to get this lyra transition	I am learning, and if I persevere, I will learn this lyra transition	I will focus on finding my centre in the first part of this lyra transition
People will think I look horrible in this awful costume	People will be impressed by my skills	Focus on the feeling of the apparatus
I feel weak today, training is going to be a nightmare	Today will be a good opportunity to go over the basics	Squeeze those muscles and keep the core tight
I am useless to my circus company now that I am injured	I am a person who is a circus artist; my health is important. I will perform for my company again once I have healed	Today I will start the day with my rehabilitation exercises
My performance today was terrible	Everybody makes mistakes; my performance will be better next time	Tomorrow I am going to practise the part of my performance that did not go so well

Summary

* Both short-term and long-term goals are useful for circus artists'
  motivation and performance
* Mastery goals describe a particular outcome a circus artist wants
  to achieve that is not impacted by external factors. This goal type
  is beneficial to performance and mental health
* Avoidance goals describe undesirable outcomes a circus artist wants to avoid, and may decrease motivation and mental
  health
* Goals are most efficient if they are set using the SMARTS
  principle

- Positive and instructional self-talk are useful to increase motivation, self-confidence, and performance
- Negative self-talk can undermine motivation, self-confidence, and performance

Exercise answers: are these goals SMARTS?

- Goal 1: is specific, measurable, and time-bound. It might be realistic and self-determined. It is not action-oriented because it does not specify what the circus artist needs to do to achieve the goal of getting the middle splits
- Goal 2: is specific, measurable, action-oriented, realistic, and time-bound. It might be self-determined
- Goal 3: is specific, measurable, and action-oriented. It might be realistic and self-determined. It is not time-bound because it does not explain when the time frame for this goal has passed: is the circus artist going to do this for eternity?
- Goal 4: is specific, measurable, and time-bound. It might be self-determined, it is unlikely to be realistic, and it is not action-oriented because it does not specify what the circus artist needs to do to lose weight. Also, this is a weight goal, not a health goal. Weight goals are not ideal in relation to body satisfaction, self-confidence, and disordered eating (see Chapter 5)
- Goal 5: is action-oriented, realistic, and time-bound. It might be self-determined. It is not specific because 'improve' can be interpreted in many ways. (What specifically is the circus artist trying to improve, how much improvement is required?) The term 'improve' is also not measurable. To improve this goal, it is important to focus on specific aspects of 'improvement', and how you could assess whether this improvement has occurred.

References

Adie, J. W., Duda, J. L., & Ntoumanis, N. (2010). Achievement goals, competition appraisals, and the well-being of elite youth soccer players across two competitive seasons. *Journal of Sport & Exercise Psychology, 32*, 555–579.

Benita, M., Roth, G., & Deci, E. L. (2014). When are mastery goals more adaptive? It depends on experiences of autonomy support and autonomy. *Journal of Educational Psychology, 106*(1), 258–267.

Elliot, A. J. (1999). Approach and avoidance motivation and achievement goals. *Educational Psychologist, 34*, 169–189.

Eum, K., & Rice, K. G. (2011). Test anxiety, perfectionism, goal orientation, and academic performance. *Anxiety, Stress & Coping: An International Journal, 24*, 167–178.

Halvari, H., Skjesol, K., & Bagøien, T. E. (2011). Motivational climates, achievement goals, and physical education outcomes: A longitudinal test of achievement goal theory. *Scandinavian Journal of Educational Research*, *55*(1), 79–104.

Hatzigeorgiadis, A., Zourbanos, N., Galanis, E., & Theodorakis, Y. (2011). Self-talk and sports performance: A meta-analysis. *Perspectives on Psychological Science*, *6*(4), 348–356.

Hatzigeorgiadis, A., Zourbanos, N., Mpoumpaki, S., & Theodorakis, Y. (2009). Mechanisms underlying the self-talk–performance relationship: The effects of motivational self-talk on self-confidence and anxiety. *Psychology of Sport and Exercise*, *10*(1), 186–192.

Lochbaum, M., & Gottardy, J. (2015). A meta-analytic review of the approach-avoidance achievement goals and performance relationships in the sport psychology literature. *Journal of Sport and Health Science*, *4*(2), 164–173.

Kuster, M., Backes, S., Brandstätter, V., Nussbeck, F. W., Bradbury, T. N., Sutter-Stickel, D., & Bodenmann, G. (2017). Approach-avoidance goals and relationship problems, communication of stress, and dyadic coping in couples. *Motivation and Emotion*, *41*(5), 576–590.

Tenenbaum, G., Pinchas, S., Elbaz, G., Bar-Eli, M., & Weinberg, R. (1991). Effect of goal proximity and goal specificity on muscular endurance performance: A replication and extension. *Journal of Sport and Exercise Psychology*, *13*(2), 174–187.

Van Dyke, E. D., Van Raalte, J. L., Mullin, E. M., & Brewer, B. W. (2018). Self-talk and competitive balance beam performance. *The Sport Psychologist*, *32*(1), 33–41.

Van Raalte, J. L., Vincent, A., & Brewer, B. W. (2016). Self-talk: Review and sport-specific model. *Psychology of Sport and Exercise*, *22*, 139–148.

Van Yperen, N. W., Elliot, A. J., & Anseel, F. (2009). The influence of mastery-avoidance goals on performance improvement. *European Journal of Social Psychology*, *39*(6), 932–943.

Wegner, D. M. (1989). *White bears and other unwanted thoughts*. New York: Viking/Penguin.

Weinberg, R. (2010). Making goals effective: A primer for coaches. *Journal of Sport Psychology in Action*, *1*(2), 57–65.

Weinberg, R., & Gould, D. (2019). Goal setting. In: *Foundations of sport and exercise psychology* (pp. 361–380). Champaign, IL: Human Kinetics.

Woodman, T., Barlow, M. D., & Gorgulu, R. (2015). Don't miss, don't miss, d'oh! Performance when anxious suffers specifically where least desired. *Sport Psychologist*, *29*(3), 213–223.

8   Mental imagery in circus

Understanding mental imagery

Mental imagery is a mental skill in which a person deliberately uses their senses to create an imagined experience that is as close as possible to a real experience (Pavlik & Nordin-Bates, 2016). Mental imagery is sometimes called 'visualisation', but this term can be confusing because it implies that imagery only involves the sense of sight. Instead, the effective use of mental imagery is multisensory; it involves using all senses. For example, a circus artist may use mental imagery to reduce their performance anxiety by imagining the start of their aerial silks act as described in Textbox 8.1.

TEXTBOX 8.1 Example of imagery to reduce performance anxiety.

As I step onto the stage, I feel nervous. The room is dark. I feel the texture of the wooden stage floor underneath my bare feet. I hear a slight murmur coming from the audience. As always, I give my silks a strong pull. I can feel the familiar texture of the silks on my fingertips. My chest expands as I take a deep breath in, I can smell the rosin on my hands. Slowly, I breathe out. My nerves start to fade away and I feel in control. I begin to climb the silks, and feel my strong muscles work as I climb to my starting position. I know I am ready to start my act, and I give the crew a thumbs up. They turn on the spotlight, and I notice the warmth of the bright light on my skin. I hear the first notes of the music of my act. I feel confident that I am going to perform well.

DOI: 10.4324/9781003289227-11

Mental imagery is a powerful mental skill. It can make people feel as though they are actually experiencing an event, rather than just imagining it. It can even produce mental and physiological outcomes that are very similar to what the person would experience if they were actually experiencing the event (Kosslyn, Thompson, & Ganis, 2006). An extreme example of this – which most people can relate to – is dreaming. Even though dreams are imagined events, a nightmare can cause us to wake up covered in sweat and with a racing heart. A delightful dream can make us feel happy and upbeat for hours after we have woken up. With practice, purposeful mental imagery can have similar effects.

Consistently, research shows that mental imagery can improve performance in sport and performing arts such as music (see Simonsmeier & Buecker, 2017; Wright, Wakefield, & Smith, 2014). In gymnastics, mental imagery has the greatest impact on performance when gymnasts use imagery at the end of a training session. The same study also shows that imagery impacts the performance of high-level gymnasts more compared to lower-level gymnasts (Simonsmeier et al., 2018). Recently, researchers have also become interested in the capacity of mental imagery to increase physical capabilities (such as strength). Although this research is still developing, Reiser, Büsch, and Munzert (2011) found that adding imagined strength training to a physical strength training programme can increase strength gains, even if the time spent on physical strength training is slightly reduced. Mental imagery may also be beneficial during rehabilitation to improve functional mobility of people who are injured (Zach et al., 2018). That said, more research is required to understand how and when this works. Regardless, imagery plays an important role during rehabilitation. It has been found to decrease perceived pain and increase self-efficacy among injured athletes (Zach et al., 2018). Taken together, imagery is an important mental skill that can contribute to thriving in circus, which is why it is useful to understand the purposes of mental imagery for circus artists.

Purposes of mental imagery for circus artists

Broadly speaking, the purposes of imagery can be classified into two categories. The most commonly known purpose of mental imagery is cognitive imagery. Cognitive imagery describes the use of mental imagery with the goal of practising or improving skills and routines. For example, a circus artist might use mental imagery to practise a complex wrap in the aerial silks, or to memorise their tightwire routine. The benefit of this is that the artist can practise their skills without physically exhausting themselves. Research shows that the use of cognitive imagery improves the performance of gymnasts (Simon-smeier et al., 2018). There is still much to learn about how mental imagery works exactly (Moran et al., 2012). However, PET scans show that when we think of moving our muscles, almost identical parts of the brain are used as when a person actually executes the movement (Malouin et al., 2003). This could mean that practising a skill using mental imagery could strengthen the same neuropathways in the brain as when a person actually executes the skill.

The second purpose of mental imagery is motivational imagery. This type of imagery is used to experience positive feelings, such as imagining achieving your goals and changing unwanted feelings (such as anxiety) into positive ones (such as confidence). In these types of imagery scenarios, people imagine themselves in a perfor-mance setting, imagine how they would usually feel this scenario (for example, anxious) and then imagine themselves successfully dealing with these feelings. Sometimes, psychologists will even introduce biofeedback into these imagery scenarios, where the circus artist would, for example, wear a heart rate monitor, and the psycholo-gist monitors whether their heart rate goes up when they imagine the event that provokes anxiety, and whether they are able to bring their heart rate back down as they imagine dealing with their feel-ings successfully. Research has shown that effective use of motiva-tional imagery can reduce performance anxiety among performing artists (Osborne, Greene, & Immel, 2014), while it can also improve performance (Short et al., 2002). Textbox 8.2 – at the end of this chapter – provides an example of a motivational imagery script with the purpose of achieving relaxation.

Testing and building your imagery ability

The higher a person's imagery ability, the more effective their men-tal imagery will be in achieving its purpose (Simonsmeier & Buecker, 2017). To maximise the effect of mental imagery, it is therefore impor-tant to take the time to develop your imagery ability. One crucial com-ponent of imagery ability is the level of imagery vividness a person can achieve. Imagery vividness refers to the strength and clarity of mental imagery, in relation to experiencing each of the senses relevant to the mental imagery. The stronger your imagery vividness, the more effec-tive your imagery session will be (Simonsmeier & Buecker, 2017). For physical tasks, such as executed by athletes, dancers, and circus art-ists, the ability to have vivid kinaesthetic imagery (sometimes called motor imagery) is particularly important (Monsma & Overby, 2004). Kinaesthetic imagery describes a person's ability to experience how their body feels when they would be executing a skill in real life (for example, muscle contraction).

To test the vividness component of your imagery ability, you can do a simple exercise prior to starting a training session. In this exercise, you imagine yourself executing a specific circus skill that you can comfortably do. Then, you answer the following questions. What does your body feel like when you execute this skill (muscle activation, pressure against body parts, etc.)? What do you see when you execute this skill? What background noise can you hear? What does the apparatus/floor feel like when you execute the skill (texture, weight, etc.)? What smells do you smell (particularly useful when it comes to performance venues)? Is there a specific taste you might taste when you execute the skill? After answering these questions, you physically execute the skill a few times, paying attention to all of these sensations. The differences you experienced between your imagined attempt and the real attempt provide clues about your imagery ability. Smaller differences represent higher levels of imagery ability. After having executed the skill a few times, imagine executing the skill again. Most people would say they feel that their imagery vividness has improved compared to their first attempt. It can also be fun to do an exercise to assess imagery vividness using food (oranges or cold cooked spaghetti works quite well). In the food-related exercise, you first imagine what it would be like to touch, squeeze, smell, and eat the food. Once you have imagined this, you bring out the food, and pay attention to what it is like to actually touch, squeeze, smell, and eat the food. Once you are done, you work on something else for a little while, and then imagine touching, squeezing, smelling, and eating the same food again. This too provides an excellent exercise to test (and even improve on) imagery vividness. Some people with high levels of imagery vividness even start salivating when they imagine eating the food!

The second crucial component of imagery ability is imagery controllability. This refers to a circus artist's ability to change what they experience in their imagery attempt. For example, a circus artist might use imagery to work on their ability to correctly execute their act, because they are making mistakes in their positioning on stage. In this scenario, it is likely that the circus artist makes similar mistakes during imagery, where they imagine themselves at the wrong part of the stage. A circus artist with high levels of imagery controllability will be able to change what they imagine (the mistake) to the desired behaviour (where they should actually be on stage). Imagery controllability is a very important skill, because if someone imagines themselves failing, this has a negative impact on performance (Short et al., 2002). While if people imagine themselves being successful, this has a positive effect on performance. In other words, when circus artists are not able to control their imagery, their well-intentioned attempts to engage in imagery might reduce their performance, for example, if they imagine themselves making mistakes.

To test your imagery controllability, it is best to choose a topic that cannot impact your performance. For example, imagine your bedroom (if you are in your bedroom right now, imagine a different room you are very familiar with). Now that you have the room clear in your mind, can you imagine the walls being a different colour? The texture of the floor feeling differently under your bare feet? A different scent than usual in the room? The door to the room being in a different place? The more things you can change in your mind, the better your imagery controllability.

Building your imagery ability is no easy feat. It requires practice. Doing the vividness and controllability exercises described in this chapter is a good start. However, if a circus artist is very keen to improve their imagery ability for the purpose of performance enhancement, it is best that they get in touch with a qualified (sport or performance) psychologist. The reason why seeking support is better than trying to do it yourself is that imagery gone wrong can negatively affect your performance. Working with a professional is the safest way to improve your imagery skills. Both group workshops and individual sessions can be quite effective in improving imagery ability, and of course, group sessions are usually more cost-effective than individual sessions. Inviting a psychologist to work on mental imagery with a group of circus artists in a few workshops, can be an excellent start to help circus artists improve their mental skills.

Creating effective mental imagery scripts for circus

The effectiveness of mental imagery on its envisioned outcome does not only depend on a circus artist's imagery vividness and controllability. The quality of the imagery script used by the artist also impacts imagery effectiveness. An imagery script is a text that is designed to guide the circus artist in their imagery.

Research has shown 'PETTLEP' can be used to maximise the effectiveness of an imagery script. PETTLEP is an acronym, and the more components of PETTLEP are covered in the delivery of an imagery script, the more effective the imagery is likely to be (Holmes & Collins, 2001).

- The first P of PETTLEP stands for *Physical*, where an imagery script is most effective if you can mimic – from a physical perspective – the 'real-life' situation as much as possible. For example, if a circus artist is usually standing in their act, the circus artist could be standing during imagery as well. The circus artist may even make small movements throughout their imagery experience to represent the imagined movements

- The first E of PETTLEP stands for *Environment*. It can be helpful to do mental imagery in the environment the artist will perform in, perhaps holding their apparatus, and maybe even listening to the music they use. The closer you can get to the circus environment that is relevant to the purpose of the imagery script, the better

- The first T of PETTLEP stands for *Task*. When creating an imagery script, it is important that the script is relevant to the circus artists' role. For example, doing a ground acrobatics imagery script with a circus artist who never performs ground acrobatics makes little sense. Also, the task should be relevant to the circus artists' skill level. Ideally, an imagery script is exactly at their ability level, or slightly beyond their current level. If the task is unattainable for the circus artist (for example, a circus artist imagining landing a triple somersault off the teeterboard while they can barely do a single somersault), the imagery script will not be effective in enhancing performance

- The second T stands for *Timing*. If the purpose of the imagery script is to increase performance, imagining the task in real time is beneficial. This is even more important when timing is important in successful skill execution, which is the case in many circus disciplines.

- The L stands for *Learning*. The most effective imagery scripts are constantly revised to match the progress and learning of the circus artists.

- The second E stands for *Emotion*. For motivational imagery (such as gaining confidence and managing arousal levels), it is important that emotions are mentioned in the imagery script. For example, the imagery script may start with 'As you walk onto the stage you feel nervous'. Then, the imagery script includes how the circus artist successfully deals with these emotions. For example 'you take a deep breath in and out, and the nerves fade away'. In cognitive imagery scripts, it can also be useful to include emotions, because it may make the imagery script more realistic to the circus artist.

- The last P of PETTLEP stands for *Perspective*. When a circus artist does imagery, they can adopt either an internal or external imagery perspective. If the circus artist uses internal imagery, they experience imagery through their own eyes. If the circus artist uses external imagery, they experience imagery as though they are watching themselves projected on a screen. Dependent on the purpose of the imagery script, both internal and external imagery perspectives can be useful. An internal imagery perspective has a broad scope of use. It is useful when a circus artist is doing imagery to feel the sensation of movement, or to feel their emotions. For example, internal imagery is useful to practise the flow of fluid transitions in sequences of skills. External imagery is useful when a circus artist is using imagery to correct errors in form or posture. For example, external imagery can be used to make a circus artist aware of a bent leg, and to use imagery to practise straightening the leg when performing the skill. People with high levels of imagery controllability are able to switch imagery perspectives when requested.

Example of a motivational imagery script for relaxation

This chapter shows that mental imagery is a powerful mental skill that can be used for a range of different purposes. Many factors impact the effectiveness of imagery in achieving the desired outcome. Some are specific to the circus artist, while other factors are related to the effectiveness of the imagery script and the way it is delivered. Because many factors impact on the effectiveness of imagery, it is important that imagery scripts are tailored as much as possible to the abilities and needs of the circus artist. This makes it difficult to provide an example of a circus-specific imagery script that is relevant and safe to use for all readers of this book. To still give you the opportunity to experience imagery, Textbox 8.2 provides an example of a motivational imagery script that aims to increase relaxation. This script is deliberately generic and not circus-specific, to increase the chances that it is relevant to as many readers as possible, while decreasing the chances that it has a negative impact on people's performance.

TEXTBOX 8.2 Imagery relaxation script.

Before starting this imagery script, I would like you to find yourself a comfortable position. When you are comfortable, I want you to close your eyes. Now, take a couple of deep breaths in, and out, and in, and out. In this imagery script, you are going to experience a relaxing day at the beach.

Imagine yourself at the top of some wooden stairs, these stairs will lead you to the beach. It is a beautiful day, the sky is blue,

---

(Continued)

and you can feel the warm sensation of the sun on your skin. There is a comfortable sea breeze, and you can smell the familiar scent of the ocean.

When you are ready, I would like you to slowly take your first step down the stairs. Notice the feeling in your legs as you make this step. Now slowly walk all the way down the stairs while paying attention to the feeling in your leg muscles.

Now that you have arrived at the bottom of the stairs, I want you to take a look at your feet. If you are wearing shoes or flip-flops, please take them off now. You step into the sand and wiggle your toes. Feel the sensation of the sand between your toes. The sand is nice and warm.

You take a look at the ocean, and hear the comforting sound of the calm waves. It is making you feel relaxed. Notice the pleasant feeling of the sun's rays on your head. Slowly, you start walking towards the ocean. Feel the muscles in your calves work as you walk through the sand. You stop walking and notice a beautiful seashell in the sand. You bend to pick the seashell up, feel the texture of the shell as you touch it.

You look around you, the beach is empty. But in the distance, you notice a beach chair. It is there especially for you. Slowly, you walk towards the beach chair, noticing your leg muscles work as you walk through the sand. You can hear the sound of a seagull as it flies over.

Now that you have arrived at the beach chair, I would like you to take a seat. Next to the chair, there is a cooling box, which has been brought there for you. You open it, and see your favourite drink. You grab the drink and smoothly open it. Take a moment to enjoy the taste of your favourite drink while listening to the sound of the waves. Notice the pleasantly warm feeling of the sun. You feel calm and relaxed.

Now that you have finished your drink, you put it back into the cooling box. You look up at the sky, and notice one small white cloud. In the distance, you hear the sound of a seagull. Slowly, you get up from the beach chair. You gently stretch yourself, and notice how nice the slight stretch makes your muscles feel. You smile, you are enjoying your relaxing day at the beach.

This script should be read slowly, with pauses between each sentence. This gives people time to experience each imagery component described. Make sure the imagery script is delivered in a quiet space.

Summary

- Mental imagery is a powerful mental skill that involves using all of the senses to create an imagined event that is as close as possible to a real event
- Mental imagery can improve performance in circus
- Mental imagery can be used with the purpose to practise and improve skills (cognitive imagery) and with the purpose to regulate arousal and emotions (motivational imagery)
- To maximise the effect of mental imagery, it is important for circus artists to have high levels of imagery ability, such as controllability and vividness
- Imagery ability can be improved with practice
- Imagery scripts are created to help guide circus artists through their mental imagery
- PETTLEP can be used to maximise the efficiency of an imagery script

References

Holmes, P. S., & Collins, D. J. (2001). The PETTLEP approach to motor imagery: A functional equivalence model for sport psychologists. *Journal of Applied Sport Psychology, 13*(1), 60–83.

Kosslyn, S. M., Thompson, W. L., & Ganis, G. (2006). *The case for mental imagery.* New York: Oxford University Press.

Malouin, F., Richards, C. L., Jackson, P. L., Dumas, F., & Doyon, J. (2003). Brain activations during motor imagery of locomotor-related tasks: A PET study. *Human Brain Mapping, 19*(1), 47–62.

Monsma, E. V., & Overby, L. Y. (2004). The relationship between imagery and competitive anxiety in ballet auditions. *Journal of Dance Medicine & Science, 8*(1), 11–18.

Moran, A., Guillot, A., MacIntyre, T., & Collet, C. (2012). Re-imagining motor imagery: Building bridges between cognitive neuroscience and sport psychology. *The British Journal of Psychology, 103*(2), 224–247.

Osborne, M. S., Greene, D. J., & Immel, D. T. (2014). Managing performance anxiety and improving mental skills in conservatoire students through performance psychology training: A pilot study. *Psychology of Well-Being, 4*(1), 1–17.

Pavlik, K., & Nordin-Bates, S. (2016). Imagery in dance: A literature review. *Journal of Dance Medicine & Science, 20*(2), 51–63.

Reiser, M., Büsch, D., & Munzert, J. (2011). Strength gains by motor imagery with different ratios of physical to mental practice. *Frontiers in Psychology, 2*, 194.

Short, S. E., Bruggeman, J. M., Engel, S. G., Marback, T. L., Wang, L. J., Willadsen, A., & Short, M. W. (2002). The effect of imagery function and imagery direction on self-efficacy and performance on a golf putting task. *The Sport Psychologist, 16*, 48–67.

Simonsmeier, B. A., & Buecker, S. (2017). Interrelations of imagery use, imagery ability, and performance in young athletes. *Journal of Applied Sport Psychology, 29*(1), 32–43.

Simonsmeier, B. A., Frank, C., Gubelmann, H., & Schneider, M. (2018). The effects of motor imagery training on performance and mental representation of 7- to 15-year-old gymnasts of different levels of expertise. *Sport, Exercise, and Performance Psychology, 7*(2), 155–168.

Wright, D. J., Wakefield, C. J., & Smith, D. (2014). Using PETTLEP imagery to improve music performance: A review. *Musicae Scientiae, 18*, 448–463.

Zach, S., Dobersek, U., Inglis, V., & Tenenbaum, G. (2018). A meta-analysis of mental imagery effects on post-injury functional mobility, perceived pain, and self-efficacy. *Psychology of Sport and Exercise, 34*, 79–87.

9 Relaxation and arousal regulation in circus

Understanding arousal and arousal regulation

The term arousal describes a person's level of bodily activation. When a person experiences high levels of arousal, they feel hyped up, excited, jumpy, and oftentimes unable to sit still. A person with low levels of arousal feels extremely mellow. At its most extreme, low levels of arousal are almost a comatose-like state. Arousal is related to stress, but stress and arousal are not the same thing. The difference is that arousal is only about a person's level of bodily activity, while stress is the outcome of the appraisal of stressors in the environment and one's personal resources to deal with this stress (see Chapter 3). That said, when a person experiences high levels of stress, it is likely that they also experience high levels of arousal. Experiencing high levels of arousal is not necessarily a bad thing though, just as experiencing low levels of arousal is not necessarily a good thing. Instead, when it comes to performance, it appears that there is an optimum zone of functioning that describes the optimal level of arousal a person needs to experience to perform to the best of their abilities (Ruiz, Raglin & Hanin, 2014).

In its simplest form, the relationship between performance and arousal can be described as an inverted U shape, which is displayed in Figure 9.1 (Yerkes & Dodson, 1908).[1] At the top of the curve, circus artists have achieved their optimum zone of functioning, the perfect level of arousal to perform at the best of their abilities. To the sides of the top of the curve, circus artists experience either too low levels of arousal or too high levels of arousal to perform to the best of their abilities. The optimal level of arousal for a circus artist to perform to the best of their abilities depends on multiple factors. First, we need to consider the personality of the circus artist. For example, the optimal level of arousal for circus artists who score high on the personality trait

DOI: 10.4324/9781003289227–12

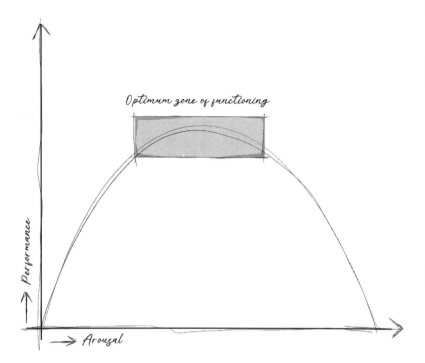

Figure 9.1 The inverted U relationship between arousal and performance. Illustration by Sharon Krisanovski.

'neuroticism' (that is, circus artists who often feel moody, anxious, and experience mood swings) tends to be lower compared to the optimal level of arousal of circus artists who score low on the personality trait neuroticism (Balyan et al., 2016). In addition to this, the amount of attention a task requires may impact the optimum zone of functioning. The performance of circus skills that are simple to the artists, that do not require much attention, or that mainly involve brute strength will likely benefit from higher levels of arousal (see Salatto et al., 2020). The ideal level of arousal to attain the optimum zone of functioning for the performance of complex skills that require much concentration and attention (such as complex juggling patterns) is expected to be lower. Together, this means that it is important to identify the optimum zone of functioning for individual circus artists based on their personality, in relation to the circus disciplines in which they participate.

A person's heart rate, sweat gland activity, and pupil size are often used as indicators of their levels of arousal (Wang et al., 2018). These forms of so-called biofeedback make it possible to quantify a person's optimum zone of functioning. This method is not perfect or foolproof, but works as a satisfactory indicator. For example, using a smart watch that measures heart rate, a circus artist can, for instance, learn that they usually have a heart rate of about 110 bmp when training circus, but that their heart rate approximates 135 bmp when they perform the same skills on stage. This difference suggests that compared to training, their arousal levels during performance are elevated. If the same circus artist often makes mistakes during the performance of their act, but not during training, this could mean that their arousal levels during the performance of an act exceed their optimum zone of functioning. The use of arousal-regulation strategies could help lower the circus artists' arousal levels during performance. This in turn could help the circus artist achieve their optimum zone of functioning, which increases the likelihood that they will perform to the best of their abilities.

Types of arousal-regulation strategies

The goal of using arousal-regulation strategies in circus is twofold. First, it can help circus artists achieve their optimum zone of functioning when performing their act, which increases the likelihood that they perform to the best of their abilities. Second, arousal-regulation strategies can fulfil a critical role in the stress-recovery balance (see Chapter 3), thereby increasing circus artists' levels of mental health. There are many methods that circus artists can use to regulate their levels of arousal. Broadly speaking, arousal-regulation strategies can be divided up into two categories: 'somatic', and 'mind to muscle' strategies. Somatic arousal-regulation strategies use the body to regulate levels of arousal in the body and mind, while mind to muscles techniques use the mind to regulate levels of arousal in the mind and body. Different people have different preferences when it comes to their favourite arousal-regulation strategy. As a guideline though, it is most useful for circus artists to match the forms of anxiety they experience with the type of arousal regulation they use (see Maynard, Hemmings, & Warwick-Evans, 1995). This means that for circus artists who experience mostly cognitive forms of anxiety – such as worrying (see Chapter 3) – using mind to muscle techniques is likely most effective, while circus artists who experience mostly somatic forms of anxiety – such as sweating and trembling (see Chapter 3) – are likely better off using somatic relaxation techniques. As with all skills, practice makes perfect. To maximise the benefits of arousal-regulation strategies, it is important to train arousal-regulation skills.

Somatic arousal-regulation strategies for circus artists

Several somatic relaxation strategies can be useful to circus artists. This section covers three somatic arousal-regulation strategies: progressive muscle relaxation, stretching, and deep-breathing exercises. All of these strategies are intended to lower one's levels of arousal.

Progressive muscle relaxation is a somatic relaxation technique that uses conscious awareness of the difference between muscle tension and muscle relaxation to promote overall relaxation and thus decrease arousal (Jacobsen, 1929). During progressive muscle relaxation, a circus artist tenses and releases muscles in a systematic manner, either from their head working their way down to their toes, or from their toes working their way up to their head. Avoid randomly tensing and releasing muscles; it does not work as well. In progressive muscle relaxation, every muscle group will be tensed for approximately five seconds. When tensing the muscles, it is important to make an effort to feel tension, but not to tense muscles too strenuously (that is, do not tense the muscles so much that it hurts). After these five seconds of tension, the muscle is released, and the circus artist focuses on how heavy and relaxed their muscles feel.

Progressive muscle relaxation has been shown to be effective in increasing physiological and mental relaxation (Toussaint et al., 2021). It may be an especially useful arousal-regulation strategy for circus artists, because circus artists often have tight and tense muscles from performing and/or training. Bringing awareness towards this muscle tension can help release tension in the body, which in turn signals the brain to feel more relaxed. Progressive muscle relaxation has been shown to improve the sleep of dancers (McCloughan et al., 2016), and some performing artists choose to use progressive muscle relaxation as part of their bedtime routine. For healthy circus artists, the use of progressive muscle relaxation is very safe. You can try progressive muscle relaxation yourself using the example in Textbox 9.1. People who are well trained in progressive muscle relaxation can eventually reduce the length of a progressive muscle relaxation exercise to a very short duration, while still achieving the same arousal-regulation outcome. This makes it possible to use progressive muscle relaxation not only to improve sleep quality, but also to regulate arousal during circus performances.

Another popular muscle to mind relaxation strategy is yoga stretching. Research has shown that 90 minutes of yoga stretching can decrease feelings of anxiety, enhance parasympathetic nerve activity, and decrease stress hormones in healthy adults without yoga experience

TEXTBOX 9.1 Progressive muscle relaxation example.

Find a comfortable position and take a couple of deep breaths in and out.

Start by tensing the muscles in your forehead by pulling your eyebrows up as high as you can.

Hold for five seconds, and release.

Now tighten the muscles of your cheeks by smiling as wide as possible.

Hold for five seconds, and release; appreciate the softness in your face.

Now tilt your head slightly back.

Hold for five seconds, and release; feel the heaviness of your relaxed head.

Now tighten your shoulder muscles by pulling your shoulders up towards your ears.

Hold it there for five seconds, and release; feel the weight of your shoulders falling down.

Now tighten your upper back muscles by trying to make your shoulder blades touch.

Hold for five seconds, and release; enjoy the sensation of your relaxed muscles.

Now tighten your biceps as tight as you can.

Hold for five seconds, and release.

Next, tighten your triceps by extending your arms in front of you, palms up, locking your elbows.

Hold it there for five seconds, and release.

Now clench your fists tightly, tensing your hand and forearm muscles.

Hold it for five seconds, and release; enjoy the relaxed feeling in your arm muscles.

Next tighten your back muscles by slightly arching your back.

Hold it there for five seconds, and release.

Now tighten your stomach muscles by tensing them as tight as you can.

Hold it, and release; enjoy the wave of relaxation going through your muscles.

Now tighten your glutes and feel yourself raise slightly in your seat.

(Continued)

Hold it, and release; notice how you sink back into your seat.

Next tighten your thighs by clenching them together, as though you are holding a pen between your knees.

Hold it for five seconds, and release.

Now tighten your calves by pulling your toes towards your chins.

Hold it there for five seconds, and release; enjoy the feeling of relaxation in your legs.

Now tighten the muscles in your feet by curling your toes under.

Hold it there tightly, and release; enjoy the relaxed feeling of heaviness in your body.

Finally, scan your body for any muscle groups that may still be carrying tension.

If you find any, tighten these muscles groups for five seconds, and release.

Appreciate the softness of the relaxed muscles in your body.

This script should be read slowly, with pauses between each sentence. This gives people time to experience each component described. Make sure the script is delivered in a quiet space. This particular script works best if you are sitting. During any progressive muscle relaxation, keep breathing steadily and do not hold your breath. If you feel any pain while tensing a particular muscle group, stop tensing it and skip the muscle group.

(Eda & Akama, 2020). The use of 30 minutes of static stretching has also been shown to decrease feelings of anxiety, increase positive mood, and reduce reaction time in cognitive tasks (Sudo, Ando & Nagamatsu, 2015). It is thus likely that yoga stretching will be a useful arousal-regulation strategy for circus artists too. Circus artists could, for example, choose to use yoga stretching as an arousal-regulation strategy prior to performing, or before going to bed to fall asleep more quickly (Wang et al., 2016). It is worth noting that no research has looked into the effect of contortion stretching on arousal. This means that it is unclear whether contortion stretching has the same effect on arousal as yoga stretching.

Finally, deep diaphragmatic breathing is another efficient somatic strategy to reduce both physiological and psychological stress in adults (Hopper et al., 2019; Hunt et al., 2018). Interestingly, increased abilities in diaphragmic breathing have also been shown to improve healthy adults' ability to balance on one leg (Stephens et al., 2017). This means that there are multiple reasons why diaphragmic breathing can be a very useful skill for circus artists. To practise your diaphragmic breathing, find yourself a comfortable spot on the floor, and lay down on your back. You may want to use a pillow under your head, or under year knees. Place your left hand on your upper chest, and your right hand just under your lowest rib on the left side of your body. Let your right arm rest on your stomach. This right arm will allow you to feel your diaphragm move while you breathe. Now slowly breathe in through your nose, so that the hand on your stomach moves up. The hand on your chest should stay as still as possible. When you are ready, breathe out via your mouth by tightening your stomach muscles, making your right hand fall. Your left hand should again stay in the same spot; your chest should not move. This breathing technique can be a bit tiring the first few times when you use it. As you get better at it, it will start to become more effortless. Once you are comfortable with deep diaphragmatic breathing while laying down, you can practise this breathing technique sitting and standing.

Although arousal-regulation strategies are usually used by performing artists and athletes to bring arousal levels down and to evoke feelings of relaxation, occasionally circus artists may need to increase their arousal levels to perform in their optimum zone of functioning. A simple muscle to mind strategy that can be used to increase arousal is engaging in forms of exercising, such as running and jumping.

Mind to muscle arousal-regulation strategies for circus artists

There are also several mind to muscle techniques that can be used by circus artists to regulate their arousal levels. The three mind to muscle arousal-regulation strategies discussed in this book are mental imagery, mindfulness, and pre-performance routines.

The mental skill mental imagery was introduced in Chapter 8. In this chapter you can find more information about what mental imagery is, and how to use mental imagery in an efficient manner. Research has shown that mental imagery can increase physiological and mental relaxation (Toussaint et al., 2021). When mental imagery is used for arousal regulation, it is useful to imagine either a situation the circus artist finds relaxing (such as a day at the beach, see Textbox 8.2), or to imagine themselves dealing successfully with stressful situations. For example, a circus artist who may struggle with the pressure of performing in front of a large audience could use mental imagery to practise performing in front of a large audience in their mind, and see themselves being successful in managing this pressure. As a result of these imagined practice sessions, circus artists will generally feel more confident in their ability to deal with pressure, and are more likely to perform to the best of their abilities when the actual event takes place.

Mindfulness is another popular mind to muscle technique used to regulate arousal levels. Mindfulness is especially useful when a person is experiencing high levels of arousal over a long time, or if a person is experiencing chronic stress. Using mindfulness, a person brings their attention to experiencing the present moment, accepting any thoughts or sensations within that present moment with openness and curiosity (Bishop et al., 2004; Van Dam et al., 2018). Scientific research about the benefits of mindfulness has rapidly evolved over the past decade, and is starting to show that the use of mindfulness-based techniques can reduce stress and increase mental health indicators such as reducing levels of depression and anxiety (Dunning et al., 2019; Poissant et al., 2020). Research has also shown that participation in performing arts such as dance can evoke experiences of mindfulness (Marich & Howell, 2015). Once circus artists learn what mindfulness is, some may realise that they experience mindfulness while doing circus. That said, it is equally possible for circus artists not to experience mindfulness while participating in circus. Circus artists are less likely to experience mindfulness during participation in circus when they experience circus-related stressors (see Chapter 3) or pain (such as injured circus artists) while doing circus. Given that professional circus artists are more likely to experience circus-related stressors compared to recreational circus artists, it is important that they do not solely rely on mindfulness experiences associated with circus, but that they also develop other arousal-regulation strategies. Importantly, circus artists can deliberately implement mindfulness techniques in their daily lives by using a structured and strategic approach to improve well-being. An example of this is using the core principles of Acceptance and Commitment Therapy (ACT; Hayes, Strosahl, & Wilson, 2009). ACT consists of six core principles, namely acceptance, cognitive defusion, being present, self as context, values, and committed action.

The first and arguably most important principle of ACT is acceptance. This means that the circus artist accepts that things will sometimes get difficult, that negative situations do exist, and that you cannot be your best self at all times. It requires a circus artist to accept that some stressful situations are beyond their control, instead of fighting or avoiding the unchangeable. For example, a circus artist who got rejected after doing an audition for a show may accept that yes, this situation makes them feel hurt, sad, and worried. The second, cognitive diffusion, principle is focused on responding to negative experiences. ACT recommends circus artists face negative experiences without fixating on them, knowing that it is okay to experience negative emotions. This will allow the circus artist to experience the third principle of ACT, to become more present in the current moment, and to experience the current moment without trying to predict or change the experience. Within this, circus artists will see themselves as the context of the experience, which is the fourth principle of ACT. In the current example, this means that the circus artist realises that the experience of what happens to them is also part of them. However, they are also aware that they are more than just the failed attempt at getting casted in a show (for example, they are a hard worker, a great performer, a kind person, etc.). The fifth principle of ACT explains that the circus artist will reflect on their values, and what they find important. The circus artist can do this by brainstorming and making a long list of things that matter to them. This could include circus-related values such as sending a particular message through their art, challenging themselves to learn something new, and being a reliable base for their flyer. But these values should also extend beyond circus, such as being a role model for their children, bringing joy, connecting people, ... The sky is the limit when it comes to values, and every circus artist will have different values. Based on these values, the circus artist can then take committed action (sixth principle of ACT), by focusing on something within their control that relates to their values. The circus artist from the example – who just experienced a rejection after an audition – may value being a role model to their child. For this reason, they may decide to take action by showing their child how life can knock you down, and that it is okay to feel upset about this. At the same time, the circus artist may want to show that this does not mean they have to give up, by persevering and getting ready for the next audition. Taking action can also look completely differently though. For example, the same circus artist may decide to take committed action by making time to spend with their child. There are no rights or wrongs in taking committed action as long as the action relates to the circus artist's values.

Finally, circus artists may choose to develop pre-performance routines to regulate their levels of arousal. This involves a circus artist systematically engaging in a self-paced, pre-set routine of actions prior to performing a skill (Moran, 1996). These actions are designed to regulate arousal by giving the circus artist a sense of control over the situation. This means that different circus artists will benefit from different pre-performance routines, and that they may have different pre-performance routines based on the circus discipline they are about to do (Clowes & Knowles, 2013). A pre-performance routine can include many different actions, and can be relevant to a variety of situations. For example, a circus artist may have a pre-performance routine prior to the start of a show that includes a pre-set routine of stretching, nutrition, hydration, and organising their costumes in a particular way. Similarly, a circus artist may also have a short pre-performance routine prior to executing a big trick. This may include taking a few deep breaths (see somatic arousal-regulation strategies section in this chapter), using a self-determined motivational cue word relevant to performance (for example, thinking of the word 'strong' just before performing that big strength-based trick), or using a five-second countdown prior to the performance of the skill (Mesagno & Mullane-Grant, 2010). Research has shown that the use of pre-performance routines decreases experiences of performance anxiety and improves performance under pressure in sport (Hazell, Cotterill, & Hill, 2014). It is likely that pre-performance routines have similar beneficial effects for circus artists.

Creating circus shows with the optimum zone of functioning in mind

Although some circus artists have the mental skills to regulate their arousal levels to achieve their optimal zones of functioning no matter what situation they find themselves in, this may not be the case for all circus artists on all occasions. It is quite common that circus artists perform multiple acts in a show, and for this reason, it is important to consider circus artists' optimum zones of functioning during the creation of a show. For example, a juggler's optimum zone of functioning is likely in a low range of arousal. Requiring a juggler to be part of a dance act seconds before performing their juggling act will increase the juggler's levels of arousal, potentially exceeding the juggler's optimum zone of functioning, and thus increasing the chances of the juggler making mistakes and dropping an object. Instead, it would be useful for the juggler to have a bit of time to bring their arousal levels down, by being able to go backstage or to only serve as a 'prop' on stage. The opposite is the case for a circus artist who is required to perform at the maximum range of their strength. This artist might struggle to achieve sufficient levels of arousal to attain their optimum zone of functioning when they are required to be a 'prop' on stage and to stand or sit still for a long period of time just prior to executing their skills. In this scenario, it is likely useful to give the circus artist a bit of time to increase their arousal levels backstage, or to let this circus artist do some movements that increase their arousal levels in the lead up to the strength skill that requires high levels of arousal. As mentioned at the start of this chapter, the circus artist's personality plays a crucial role in their optimum zone of functioning. This means that there are differences in the arousal levels circus artists need to perform to the best of their abilities. Once circus artists know what their optimum zone of functioning is, it is incredibly useful to ask them what they need to achieve their optimum zone of functioning, so that they have a greater opportunity to perform at their best on stage and in training.

Summary

- The term arousal describes a person's level of bodily activity
- The 'inverted U curve' explains the core relationship between arousal levels and performance
- To perform to the best of their abilities, it is important that circus artists can reach their optimum zone of functioning
- Circus artists' optimum zones of functioning vary based on their personality and circus-specific factors
- Somatic arousal-regulation techniques can be used to decrease arousal. These include progressive muscle relaxation, stretching, and deep breathing
- Mind to muscle techniques can also be used to regulate arousal in circus. These include mental imagery, mindfulness, and pre-performance routines

Note

1 The inverted U hypothesis provides an excellent first step in understanding how arousal affects performance. The 'Cusp Catastrophe model' (Hardy & Parfitt, 1991) is a more comprehensive model to predict performance. This rather complex model bases its performance predictions on the intricate relationships among cognitive anxiety, arousal, and performance. You can learn more about this by reading: Hardy, L., & Parfitt, G. (1991). A catastrophe model of anxiety and performance. *British Journal of Psychology, 82*(2), 163–178.

References

Balyan, K. Y., Tok, S., Tatar, A., Binboga, E., & Balyan, M. (2016). The relationship among personality, cognitive anxiety, somatic anxiety, physiological arousal, and performance in male athletes. *Journal of Clinical Sport Psychology, 10*(1), 48–58.

Bishop, S. R., Lau, M., Shapiro, S., Carlson, L., Anderson, N. D., Carmody, J., Segal, Z. V., Abbey, S., Speca, M., Velting, D., & Devins, G. (2004). Mindfulness: A proposed operational definition. *Clinical Psychology: Science and Practice, 11*(3), 230–241.

Clowes, H., & Knowles, Z. (2013). Exploring the effectiveness of pre-performance routines in elite artistic gymnasts: A mixed method investigation. *Science of Gymnastics Journal, 5*(2), 27–40.

Dunning, D. L., Griffiths, K., Kuyken, W., Crane, C., Foulkes, L., Parker, J., & Dalgleish, T. (2019). Research review: The effects of mindfulness-based interventions on cognition and mental health in children and adolescents – A meta-analysis of randomized controlled trials. *Journal of Child Psychology and Psychiatry, 60*(3), 244–258.

Eda, N., Ito, H., & Akama, T. (2020). Beneficial effects of yoga stretching on salivary stress hormones and parasympathetic nerve activity. *Journal of Sports Science and Medicine, 19*(4), 695–702.

Hayes, S. C., Strosahl, K. D., & Wilson, K. G. (2009). *Acceptance and commitment therapy.* Washington, DC: American Psychological Association.

Hazell, J., Cotterill, S. T., & Hill, D. M. (2014). An exploration of pre-performance routines, self-efficacy, anxiety and performance in semi-professional soccer. *European Journal of Sport Science, 14*(6), 603–610.

Hopper, S. I., Murray, S. L., Ferrara, L. R., & Singleton, J. K. (2019). Effectiveness of diaphragmatic breathing for reducing physiological and psychological stress in adults: A quantitative systematic review. *JBI Evidence Synthesis, 17*(9), 1855–1876.

Hunt, M. G., Rushton, J., Shenberger, E., & Murayama, S. (2018). Positive effects of diaphragmatic breathing on physiological stress reactivity in varsity athletes. *Journal of Clinical Sport Psychology, 12*(1), 27–38.

Jacobsen, E. (1929). *Progressive relaxation*. Chicago, IL: University of Chicago Press.

Marich, J., & Howell, T. (2015). Dancing mindfulness: A phenomenological investigation of the emerging practice. *Explore*, *11*(5), 346–356.

Maynard, I. W., Hemmings, B., & Warwick-Evans, L. (1995). The effects of a somatic intervention strategy on competitive state anxiety and performance in semiprofessional soccer players. *The Sport Psychologist*, *9*(1), 51–64.

McCloughan, L. J., Hanrahan, S. J., Anderson, R., & Halson, S. R. (2016). Psychological recovery: Progressive muscle relaxation (PMR), anxiety, and sleep in dancers. *Performance Enhancement & Health*, *4*(1–2), 12–17.

Mesagno, C., & Mullane-Grant, T. (2010). A comparison of different pre-performance routines as possible choking interventions. *Journal of Applied Sport Psychology*, *22*(3), 343–360.

Poissant, H., Moreno, A., Potvin, S., & Mendrek, A. (2020). A meta-analysis of mindfulness-based interventions in adults with attention-deficit hyperactivity disorder: Impact on ADHD symptoms, depression, and executive functioning. *Mindfulness*, *11*, 2669–2681.

Ruiz, M. C., Raglin, J. S., & Hanin, Y. L. (2017). The individual zones of optimal functioning (IZOF) model (1978–2014): Historical overview of its development and use. *International Journal of Sport and Exercise Psychology*, *15*(1), 41–63.

Salatto, R. W., Arevalo, J. A., Brown, L. E., Wiersma, L. D., & Coburn, J. W. (2020). Caffeine's effects on an upper-body resistance exercise workout. *The Journal of Strength & Conditioning Research*, *34*(6), 1643–1648.

Stephens, R. J., Haas, M., Moore III, W. L., Emmil, J. R., Sipress, J. A., & Williams, A. (2017). Effects of diaphragmatic breathing patterns on balance: a preliminary clinical trial. *Journal of Manipulative and Physiological Therapeutics*, *40*(3), 169–175.

Sudo, M., Ando, S., & Nagamatsu, T. (2015). Effects of acute static stretching on visual search performance and mood state. *Journal of Physical Education and Sport*, *15*(4), 651–656.

Toussaint, L., Nguyen, Q. A., Roettger, C., Dixon, K., Offenbächer, M., Kohls, N.,... & Sirois, F. (2021). Effectiveness of progressive muscle relaxation, deep breathing, and guided imagery in promoting psychological and physiological states of relaxation. *Evidence-Based Complementary and Alternative Medicine*, 5924040.

Van Dam, N. T., van Vugt, M. K., Vago, D. R., Schmalzl, L., Saron, C. D., Olendzki, A., Meissner, T., Lazar, S. W., Kerr, C. E., Gorchov, J., Fox, K. C. R., Field, B. A., Britton, W. B., Brefczynski-Lewis, J. A., & Meyer, D. E. (2018). Mind the hype: A critical evaluation and prescriptive agenda for research on mindfulness and meditation. *Perspectives on Psychological Science*, *13*(1), 36–61.

Wang, C. A., Baird, T., Huang, J., Coutinho, J. D., Brien, D. C., & Munoz, D. P. (2018). Arousal effects on pupil size, heart rate, and skin conductance in an emotional face task. *Frontiers in Neurology, 9,* 1029.

Wang, F., Lee, O. E. K., Feng, F., Vitiello, M. V., Wang, W., Benson, H.,... & Denninger, J. W. (2016). The effect of meditative movement on sleep quality: A systematic review. *Sleep Medicine Reviews, 30,* 43–52.

Yerkes, R. M., & Dodson, J. D. (1908). The relation of strength of stimulus to rapidity of habit-formation. *Journal of Comparative Neurology and Psychology, 18,* 459–482.

10 Psycho-perceptual motor skills and visual anticipation in circus

Attention and motor skill execution in circus

Motor skills are involved in the performance of all tasks that require a person to use their muscles. This means that motor skills are a big part of the performance of (nearly) all circus disciplines. To understand how to improve the performance of (complex) motor skills, it is important to realise that psychological factors impact the performance of motor skills alongside other factors. OPTIMAL theory brings two of these factors together by describing how both motivation and attention impact on the performance of motor skills and motor skill learning (Wulf & Lewthwaite, 2016). When motor skills are practised and performed under optimal motivational and attentional focus conditions, more effective neural connections are formed in the brain. These neural connections impact on the performance and learning of motor skills.

OPTIMAL theory proposes that from a motivation perspective, experiences of autonomy and self-confidence influence learning and performance of motor skills. If intrinsic motivation and experiences of autonomy are achieved, motor skills are learned more efficiently, and circus artists are more likely to engage in circus in the long term. The mechanisms underlying autonomy and self-confidence are discussed in Chapters 4 and 5 respectively. From an attention perspective, OPTIMAL theory describes that attentional control impacts on motor skill execution and learning. More specifically, to increase the performance of motor skills, it is important to focus one's attention on movement-related cues that are important for movement execution and to avoid distracting cues that are irrelevant to the successful execution of a motor skill. Research in juggling, gymnastics, dance, and music has consistently shown that having an internal focus during the execution of motor skills predicts poorer skill execution outcomes compared with

DOI: 10.4324/9781003289227-13

having an external or holistic focus of attention (Abdollahipour et al., 2015; Becker, Georges, & Aiken, 2019; Mornell & Wulf, 2019; Teixeira da Silva, Thofehrn Lessa, & Chiviacowsky, 2017; Zentgraf & Munzert, 2009). Therefore, it is likely useful for all circus artists to have an external or holistic focus of attention to improve their motor skill execution. This means that a circus artist would benefit from focusing their attention on relevant external factors such as their apparatus, stage marks, the beats of the music, props, etc. A hoop diver for example, would probably perform better when they focus their attention on the hoop they are about to dive through (external focus), as opposed to thinking about the angle they should make with their body (internal focus). The reason why an internal focus of attention should be avoided is that it interrupts automatic motor processes, which in turn decrease motor skill execution (Kal, Van der Kamp, & Houdijk, 2013).

The relevance of perceptual motor skills and visual anticipation in circus

Researchers are also trying to understand how psychological skills contribute to expert perceptual motor skill performance (Müller et al., 2019). Perceptual motor skills involve the use of perceptual information (such as vision) to inform the physical performance of a skill (motor skills) (see Magill & Anderson, 2021). A perceptual skill relevant to performance in many circus disciplines is the pickup of visual information. To pick up useful visual information, it is important to understand where a person is looking when they are executing a skill; this is called visual search behaviour. Barreto et al. (2021) researched the visual search behaviour of elite and super-elite gymnasts when they were performing elite skills on a mini trampoline with a vaulting table present, and without the presence of a vaulting table. The presence of a vaulting table was relevant because it makes visual search behaviour more complex. They found that the presence of a vaulting table impacted where elite gymnasts were looking during their run towards the mini trampoline, while it did not impact on the visual search behaviour of the super-elite gymnasts. This led to the conclusion that the time the gymnasts spent fixating their gaze on the right areas during the approach run to the mini trampoline could be a crucial contributor to super-elite performance, particularly when a vaulting table is present. This information is relevant to the circus context because many acrobats work with a range of obstacles during circus performance. For example, circus artists may navigate moving around other performers during their acts (for example, jumping over and under them), and may also work with relatively stationary obstacles (such as in hoop diving). Teaching circus artists how to optimise their visual search behaviour may help them to perform more complex skills, with less errors, and thus with a lower risk of getting injured. However, visual search is something that receives little attention during circus training. It may be worthwhile to dedicate more time to the development of this skill.

An important perceptual motor skill that has received attention in sports research is visual anticipation (Williams & Jackson, 2019). Visual anticipation can be described as a person's ability to pick up visual information in their immediate environment to accurately predict what will happen next, and to use this information to guide action (Runswick et al., 2018). An example of visual anticipation in circus is how a catcher 'reads' the take-off of a flyer, to determine how and where this flyer is going to land, increasing the time the catcher has available to successfully catch the flyer. In this example, the perceptual skill is the circus artist's ability to pick up visual information relevant to successful execution of the motor skill of catching (Williams & Jackson, 2019). Interestingly, being trained to execute a skill has an impact on the brain activity of a person who is observing a person who is conducting the skill (Calvo-Merino et al., 2005). This means that training a catcher's skills as a flyer could improve their abilities as a catcher (see Brenton, & Müller, 2018).

The two-stage model of visual anticipation (Morris-Binelli & Müller, 2017) explains that there are two stages in visual anticipation. In the first stage, a person picks up early, 'advance', contextual information. This contextual information could be the placement of any props on stage, or kinematic information such as the movement pattern and angle of the circus artist's body prior to take-off. The catcher uses this advance information to guide the initial positioning of their body (for example, move arms up, do a big step to the right). In the second stage of visual anticipation, the catcher looks at the flight pattern of the acrobat, and fine tunes their positioning for the optimal catch (for example, by slightly adjusting the angle of their body and arms).

Testing and training visual anticipation in circus

A method to test a person's visual anticipation skills that has been used in sport, and could be used in circus, is video-based temporal occlusion. In brief, this would involve a circus artist watching a video of a skill, in which the amount of visual information the circus artist can see is controlled by stopping the video at a specific time. For example, a circus artist may only see the first few milliseconds of an acrobat who is about to take-off from the teeterboard, and not the 'flight' of the acrobat. The artist will then, for example, be asked to predict whether the acrobat lands back onto the board. Another example of video-based temporal occlusion in circus is an artist who watches a video of a partner juggling scenario. They are shown the throw of their partner towards them, but not the flight of the juggling club. The artist is then asked to move their hand to the place where they think the club is going to land. Research in a range of sports, including rhythmic gymnastics, has shown that higher-level athletes have greater visual anticipation skills compared with lesser performers (Farrow & Reid, 2012; Kioumourtzoglou et al., 1997; Runswick et al., 2018). This means that superior visual anticipation skills could improve performance.

Importantly, research in field hockey (Morris-Binelli et al., 2021, 2022) has shown that training visual anticipation skills can improve even elite athletes' abilities of picking-up 'advance' visual information. These athletes did not only improve their abilities to predict what would happen in a video test, but some also improved their on-field performance. The way how these athletes trained their visual anticipation skills was by using a tailor-made training programme consisting of videos that used the temporal occlusion method. This means that athletes were shown videos of field hockey players shooting a ball at the goal but that the videos were stopped at different moments. These moments represented the different amounts of visual information available (for example, the video may be stopped at the moment the ball is about to leave the stick, or in the middle of ball flight). When the video was stopped, the hockey player was asked to predict where in the goal the ball was going. After they made their prediction, the athletes watched the remainder of the video, which showed where the ball ended up in the goal. Using a video-based method to train visual anticipation has a couple of benefits to circus artists. First, stopping the videos early on will implicitly guide a person to only use advance information to interpret what will happen, without explicitly telling the person where to look. This is important, because explicit learning (i.e., telling the person where to look) can negatively affect performance under pressure (Lam, Maxwell, & Masters, 2009). Second, showing the artist the 'answer' to the question they were asked will give a person immediate feedback about whether their prediction was correct. This feedback facilitates learning. Third, using videos is a very safe approach to developing visual anticipation skills, because there is no risk that mistakes lead to accidents or injuries (such as missing a catch or getting hit by a juggling club).

Aside from using traditional videos to train visual anticipation, the circus environment can also be simulated in virtual reality. The potential benefit of this method is that it allows for the presence of more contextual information. If done well, this could increase the fidelity of the experience, meaning that the experience is even closer to the 'real' experience. Using virtual reality will make it, for example, possible for circus artists to rotate their head and see what is going on around them. In virtual reality, it would thus be possible for a circus artist to train their visual anticipation skills while maintaining oversight of other things that are happening on stage at roughly the same time. Similar to sport (see Discombe et al., 2022), immersive videos could thus be an effective method to assess and train visual anticipation in circus. It would be worthwhile to set up a series of research projects with the aim of learning more about the visual anticipation skills of circus artists, and creating training programmes aimed at increasing the visual anticipation skills of circus artists in a range of circus disciplines.

The impact of psychological skills on perceptual motor skills in circus

As mentioned at the start of this chapter, psychological skills impact on the performance of perceptual motor skills. For this reason, researchers and practitioners are becoming more interested in training psycho-perceptual motor skills. The 'psycho' component in psycho-perceptual motor skills refers to the circus artists' ability to manage emotions such as stress and anxiety that are often present during circus performance (Weissensteiner et al., 2012). Managing these emotions is important, because they can impact on a person's visual field, their ability to pick up visual information, the information they have available for visual anticipation, and, ultimately, their ability to achieve a motor skill goal (Cocks et al., 2016). This means that it is important to look at psycho-perceptual motor skills together, because when combined, they impact performance (Müller et al., 2019; Zaichkowsky & Peterson, 2018).

For this reason, it is useful that the circus training environment is as similar as possible to the performance environment (often called a 'representative' environment) (Magill & Anderson, 2021). This is generally done quite well in circus. To make training representative of performance, many circus artists do not just practise skills separately, instead they practise their skills in sequences. Circus artists often listen to the music that is played during their act while they are training, which can facilitate external focus as described by OPTI-MAL theory. Another way in which circus artists (perhaps unknowingly) make their training representative of performance is by asking other artists to watch their newly made acts during training, which serves as a form of audience pressure. In addition, it may be useful to occasionally play distracting noises (such as an audience clapping) during training, or to get an artist's heart rate up right before training towards improving a skill that will be executed in a higher-pressure environment.

Summary

- While perceptual motor skills have the potential to improve circus artists' performance and safety, little is known about circus artists' perceptual motor skills
- OPTIMAL theory describes how motivation and attention impact motor skill execution
- Visual anticipation is a skill in which a person uses 'advance' visual cues to guide initial movement and further visual information to refine movement
- On average, higher skilled athletes have higher levels of perceptual motor skills compared with lower skilled athletes
- Perceptual motor skills such as visual anticipation can be trained. One method to train these skills, which is safe for use in circus, is video-based temporal occlusion
- Psychological skills impact a person's ability to execute perceptual motor skills
- Ensuring that the circus training environment is representative of the performance environment is useful in perceptual motor skill execution and learning

References

Abdollahipour, R., Wulf, G., Psotta, R., & Palomo Nieto, M. (2015). Performance of gymnastics skill benefits from an external focus of attention. *Journal of Sports Sciences, 33*(17), 1807–1813.

Barreto, J., Casanova, F., Peixoto, C., Fawver, B., & Williams, A. M. (2021). How task constraints influence the gaze and motor behaviours of elite-level gymnasts. *International Journal of Environmental Research and Public Health, 18*(13), 6941.

Becker, K. A., Georges, A. F., & Aiken, C. A. (2019). Considering a holistic focus of attention as an alternative to an external focus. *Journal of Motor Learning and Development, 7*(2), 194–203.

Brenton, J., & Müller, S. (2018). Is visual–perceptual or motor expertise critical for expert anticipation in sport? *Applied Cognitive Psychology, 32*(6), 739–746.

Calvo-Merino, B., Glaser, D. E., Grèzes, J., Passingham, R. E., & Haggard, P. (2005). Action observation and acquired motor skills: An fMRI study with expert dancers. *Cerebral Cortex, 15*(8), 1243–1249.

Cocks, A. J., Jackson, R. C., Bishop, D. T., & Williams, A. M. (2016). Anxiety, anticipation and contextual information: A test of attentional control theory. *Cognition and Emotion, 30(6)*, 1037–1048.

Discombe, R. M., Bird, J. M., Kelly, A., Blake, R. L., Harris, D. J., & Vine, S. J. (2022). Effects of traditional and immersive video on anticipation in cricket: A temporal occlusion study. *Psychology of Sport and Exercise, 58*, 102088.

Farrow, D., & Reid, M. (2012). The contribution of situational probability information to anticipatory skill. *Journal of Science and Medicine in Sport, 15*(4), 368–373.

Kal, E. C., Van der Kamp, J., & Houdijk, H. (2013). External attentional focus enhances movement automatization: A comprehensive test of the constrained action hypothesis. *Human Movement Science, 32*(4), 527–539.

Kioumourtzoglou, E., Derri, V., Mertzanidou, O., & Tzetzis, G. (1997). Experience with perceptual and motor skills in rhythmic gymnastics. *Perceptual and Motor Skills, 84*(3_suppl), 1363–1372.

Lam, W. K., Maxwell, J. P., & Masters, R. (2009). Analogy learning and the performance of motor skills under pressure. *Journal of Sport and Exercise Psychology, 31*(3), 337–357.

Magill, R. A., & Anderson, D. (2021). *Motor learning and control: Concepts and applications* (12th ed.). New York: McGraw Hill.

Mornell, A., & Wulf, G. (2019). Adopting an external focus of attention enhances musical performance. *Journal of Research in Music Education, 66*(4), 375–391.

Morris-Binelli, K., & Müller, S. (2017). Advancements to the understanding of expert visual anticipation skill in striking sports. *Canadian Journal of Behavioural Science/Revue canadienne des sciences du comportement, 49*(4), 262–268.

Morris-Binelli, K., Müller, S., van Rens, F. E. C. A., Harbaugh, A. G., & Rosalie, S. M. (2021). Individual differences in performance and learning of visual anticipation in expert field hockey goalkeepers. *Psychology of Sport and Exercise, 52*, 101829.

Morris-Binelli, K., Müller, S., van Rens, F. E. C. A., Harbaugh, A. G., & Rosalie, S. M. (2022). Individual differences and transfer of visual anticipation in expert female field hockey goalkeepers. *Optometry and Vision Science, 99*(2), 150–158.

Müller, S., van Rens, F., Brenton, J., Morris-Binelli, K., Piggott, B., Rosalie, S. M., & Burgin, M. (2019). Embedding of psycho-perceptual-motor skills can improve athlete assessment and training programs. *Journal of Expertise, 2*(1), 14–22.

Runswick, O. R., Roca, A., Williams, A. M., Bezodis, N. E., & North, J. S. (2018). The effects of anxiety and situation-specific context on perceptual–motor skill: A multi-level investigation. *Psychological Research, 82,* 708–719.

Teixeira da Silva, M., Thofehrn Lessa, H., & Chiviacowsky, S. (2017). External focus of attention enhances children's learning of a classical ballet pirouette. *Journal of Dance Medicine & Science, 21*(4), 179–184.

Weissensteiner, J. R., Abernethy, B., Farrow, D., & Gross, J. (2012). Distinguishing psychological characteristics of expert cricket batsmen. *Journal of Science and Medicine in Sport, 15*(1), 74–79.

Williams, A. M., & Jackson, R. C. (2019). Anticipation in sport: Fifty years on, what have we learned and what research still needs to be undertaken? *Psychology of Sport and Exercise, 42,* 16–24.

Wulf, G., & Lewthwaite, R. (2016). Optimizing performance through intrinsic motivation and attention for learning: The OPTIMAL theory of motor learning. *Psychonomic Bulletin and Review, 23*(5), 1382–1414.

Zaichkowsky, L., & Peterson, D. (2018). *The play makers advantage: How to raise your mental game to the next level.* New York: Gallery/Jeter Publishing.

Zentgraf, K., & Munzert, J. (2009). Effects of attentional-focus instructions on movement kinematics. *Psychology of Sport and Exercise, 10*(5), 520–525.

Epilogue

Whether you are a circus artist, coach, director, or otherwise involved in the circus industry, you have an opportunity to contribute to a circus environment that enables experiences of thriving under the big top. This book offers a foundation to help you understand what factors may impact mental health and performance in circus. Mental health can be a difficult topic to talk about. Hopefully this book has given you the courage to speak freely about your well-being, and to approach others that you think may be going through a tough time. If you think you, or someone you know, needs help, remember that general practitioners, psychologists, and psychiatrists can provide support.

As you may have noticed while reading this book, there are still many unknowns about the psychological factors that impact the mental health and performance of circus artists. To change this, it is important to be proactive, to share ideas, to do your own research, and to support the research of others. Be bold. Draw on your curiosity and creativity to continue your journey of learning more about circus psychology. Let us develop a circus environment wherein everybody gets an opportunity to thrive.

DOI: 10.4324/9781003289227–14

Index

Note: **Bold** page numbers refer to tables; *italic* page numbers refer to figures and page numbers followed by "n" denote endnotes.

For Product Safety Concerns and Information please contact our EU
representative GPSR@taylorandfrancis.com Taylor & Francis Verlag GmbH,
Kaufingerstraße 24, 80331 München, Germany

Printed and bound by CPI Group (UK) Ltd, Croydon, CR0 4YY

11/04/2025

01844010-0015